parched

parched

a memoir

HEATHER KING

Chamberlain Bros.
a member of Penguin Group (USA) Inc.
New York

CHAMBERLAIN BROS.
Published by the Penguin Group
Penguin Group (USA) Inc., 375 Hudson Street, New York,
New York 10014, USA
Penguin Group (Canada), 10 Alcorn Avenue, Toronto, Ontario M4V 3B2,
Canada (a division of Pearson Penguin Canada Inc.)
Penguin Books Ltd, 80 Strand, London WC2R 0RL, England
Penguin Ireland, 25 St Stephen's Green, Dublin 2, Ireland
(a division of Penguin Books Ltd)
Penguin Group (Australia), 250 Camberwell Road, Camberwell, Victoria
3124, Australia (a division of Pearson Australia Group Pty Ltd)
Penguin Books India Pvt Ltd, 11 Community Centre, Panchsheel Park,
New Delhi–110 017, India
Penguin Group (NZ), cnr Airborne and Rosedale Roads, Albany,
Auckland 1310, New Zealand (a division of Pearson New Zealand Ltd)
Penguin Books (South Africa) (Pty) Ltd, 24 Sturdee Avenue, Rosebank,
Johannesburg 2196, South Africa

Penguin Books Ltd, Registered Offices: 80 Strand, London
WC2R 0RL, England

An application has been submitted to register this book
with the Library of Congress.

ISBN 1-59609-081-2

Printed in the United States of America
10 9 8 7 6 5 4 3 2 1

Book design by Jaime Putorti

Names and identifying characteristics have been changed to protect the
privacy of the individuals involved.

acknowledgments

Before I started writing, I used to read other people's acknowledgments and imagine the writer as having turned out his or her book around a giant dining-room table, surrounded by warmth, cornucopias of food, and laughing friends. Now I know that writing—or at least my writing—takes place in almost pathological isolation, in a state vacillating between panic attack–level anxiety and religious ecstasy. Which is why it's a good thing I do have *some* people in my life. It's not so much that they help me write as that they give me a reason to live, which is why I'm deeply grateful to, in no particular order, Joan Biggs, Judy Horton, Terry Richey, Ann-Kristin Rothenberg, Maud Simmons, Fred Davis, Patrick Kerr, Clam Lynch, my sister Meredith, Julia Gibson, Brad Valdez, Glenn Lindsay, Toni Flynn, Jeff Behrens, Janet Moore, Timothy Arthur Brown, Timmy J. Smith, Joe Keyes, and Barbara Fleck.

Between them, the Djerassi Resident Artists Program and the Dorland Mountain Arts Colony gave me several amazing months of solitude, space, and natural beauty—which made me feel so guilty I *had* to write. Without my very sharp agent, Laurie Liss, I might never have *finally* sold my first book, and without my editor, Anna Cowles, it wouldn't be going out to the world in nearly as good a shape as it is. It's a way bigger deal for me than for them, but they graciously never let me know it.

Finally, special thanks to Ann Leary and Ellen Slezak–wonderful writers, sympathetic listeners, and funny, funny friends–who are closer to my heart and helped more than they can know.

For my parents—
who gave me life twice

There are places in the heart that do not yet
exist, and into them enters suffering that they
may have existence.

—Léon Bloy

"Sitio." (I thirst.)

—Christ, as he died on the cross.

John 19:28

prologue

For my soul is filled with evils;
my life is on the brink of the grave.
I am reckoned as one in the tomb:
I have reached the end of my strength,

like one alone among the dead;
like the slain lying in their graves . . .

—Psalm 88

It was September 1986, right after I'd returned to Boston from my week in Nashville, when my mother started calling to badger me about the party she was planning for my father's birthday. I would have gone up to New Hampshire anyway—they'd be counting on me to brighten things up—and it irritated me that she was making such a production out of it. It was also weird that she was having it at night. My parents got up so early they were ready for bed by six, and usually scheduled family gatherings to begin by one at the latest.

"Danny will even come down to pick you up," Mom cajoled. Danny? Dan, the youngest of my four brothers, was so busy being a martial-arts nut he never had time for anybody. "Oh great," I laughed, careful to keep the edge out of my voice as I looked at my bloodshot eyes in the mirror and groped for a bottle of Visine. "Is he bringing his nunchakus?"

The party was scheduled for a Saturday. That morning I came to, with the same mixture of guilt, dread, and nervous exhaustion to which I'd woken every morning for as far back as I could remember hanging over me like a pall. As usual, I was fully dressed: jeans, boots, jacket—I must have stumbled in, once again, and fallen straight into bed. My hands were hanging over the edge, curled a little, as if in self-defense, expecting a blow. I still had all ten fingers—that was good. I often woke with bruises, black eyes, or gashes to my head or knees, and fully expected one morning to find myself missing an arm, a leg . . . Well, that was the price you had to pay. It wouldn't be that bad—plenty of people were missing a limb; every life had to have a little pain in it. I was parched, my mouth, throat, and cranium on fire from the no doubt packs of cigarettes I'd smoked and untold number of life-sapping drinks I'd downed the night before. Like a vampire, my habit sucked me dry: if I ever tried to give blood, I sometimes reflected, it would come out straight vodka with little pieces of old lime and bent cocktail straws mixed in. I could easily have drunk a gallon of lemonade at one gulp, but I knew without looking that the refrigerator was empty. The refrigerator was always empty.

One thing to be grateful for—I peered gingerly to my left

to make sure—I was alone. Playing hard to get had never been my strong suit, but lately, even *I'd* been shocked by some of the people I'd brought home. One, apparently some kind of teenage runaway, had stayed a week. Another seemed to have lost his shoes. Then again, what were nice clothes? Or good grammar? Or teeth? It wasn't everyone that could see through to the core of a person, to his innate goodness and decency. I wasn't just sleeping around; it was part of my . . . ministry—part of my incessant quest, inextricably intertwined with my quest for the next drink, for The One.

Somewhere out there was the man I was destined for, and who was destined for me, and when I found him, peace would be restored, harmony would reign, and all my problems would be solved at last. I looked upon finding him as somewhat like looking for a needle in a haystack, a kind of obstacle-strewn treasure hunt, for if I knew one thing it was that the universe was a wily, withholding place, bent on foiling my best-laid plans. That's why the usual mate-snaring spots—the workplace, say, at a job commensurate with one's skills; church functions; dance halls—didn't occur to me for a moment. No, the way I figured it he'd turn up in the *least* likely place, which for the moment I'd decided was sitting at JT's Place, the old men's bar in North Station I'd taken to frequenting of a morning.

There he'd be: manly yet tender, self-deprecating yet strong, tormented yet self-possessed, a mixture of Jack Kerouac, William Burroughs, Dylan Thomas, Robert Mitchum, and Martin Luther King, Jr. Someone who saw the truth of the world; the truth of my own quirkily fragile, precious core—the male counterpart, in other words, of me. It was a long shot, JT's, sure, but . . . *I* was there. Why not some wild, smart, funny, poetic, well-built, together, sex-starved, possibly rich guy? Who, like me, also happened to enjoy sitting around a dingy bar with a bunch of wet brains downing sea breezes at eight a.m.?

I loosened my jacket—I couldn't remember the last time I'd worn pajamas—and let my gaze wander around my clutter-strewn, single-room-occupancy loft: dead plants, cracked windows, no sink, no stove—I cooked, if at all, on a hot plate. The bathroom was at the end of the hall. I was an alcoholic, I knew that, and yet to stop . . . it was impossible to describe the monumental abyss that that would mean crossing. My entire identity was tied up in drinking. Every ounce of my mental, emotional, and physical energy was devoted to drinking. My entire life revolved around drinking. And on top of that I was *physically* addicted: every neuron, every minute of the day and night, cried out for alcohol, like a plant during a drought. Not that this in the least made me want to stop. Or rather, I didn't believe I could stop and therefore I didn't allow myself to want to stop. Everybody drank! Everyone I knew, anyway. You'd drink, too, if you saw the world with as clear an eye as I did. And even I wasn't as bad as, say, . . . Blacky. The welfare/SSI guy who lived down the hall. Who sold me beers in the morning before the bars opened. Who, now that I thought about it, was basically my only . . . friend.

It was time to start the all-important gathering of my mental reserves for the day ahead, and pleading, begging, beseeching the master of the universe for a crumb of help, I shifted

now to grope my right jacket pocket. My fingers touched cellophane . . . please, please . . . flattened cardboard . . . fuck . . .
no!! Was it empty? . . . A bulge, oh thank you, thank you,
thank you: I had cigarettes. Not many, but three or four
crammed into a corner of the squished-up pack, I could tell
by the feel, enough to at least launch me on the task at hand.
I smoothed one out, fished a pack of matches from under the
pillow, and lit up, inhaling deeply. My world was a constant
series of bargains, outwittings, maneuverings, cliff-hanging
near-misses, rewards, and punishments, which was why I often experienced entire odysseys without ever leaving my bed.

Fortified by half a Winston's worth of nicotine, I prepared
for the next moment of truth. Most people my age—thirty-
three—had wallets, but in my case, when my waitressing shift
was over for the night, I simply crammed bills and change
willy-nilly into my pockets. In fact, I lived in a kind of Rip
van Winkle–like coma about many things that seemed to
come easily to normal people: health insurance, checkbooks,
wristwatches—these were concepts far beyond my ken. I told
myself I was embracing a kind of bare-bones purity, and
though this was true enough in its way, it wasn't because of
any philosophical convictions: it was because I was such a terrible drunk I didn't have any choice.

I patted myself down, heart sinking at each successive
empty pocket. I'd blown it all—sixty-two bucks and change as
I remembered—somewhere between the time I'd gotten out of
work the night before and whenever I'd rolled home. Oh
wait, here was a tiny wadded up . . . I regarded it hungrily, lying in my hand: three one-dollar bills, a nickel, and two pen-

nies. Enough for a pint of vodka at Macy's Liquor and sub-way fare. The dreaded, hateful, satanic subway fare. Because this was the hell of it—the oppressive, shrieking, unbearable hell: I had to work again. My head had cleared enough to re-member I was on for the lunch shift at Sam's Seafood Shack, the restaurant where, one more time, I'd somehow managed to find a job.

I sank back on the pillow and lit another cigarette, gazing dully into the middle distance. Through the window was the Lindemann Mental Health Center, a glorified nuthouse, and beyond that, my alma mater: Suffolk Law. I could hardly be-lieve it myself, it was such a cosmic joke, but it was true: I was technically a lawyer. I say "technically" because although I had managed to graduate with honors and pass the Massa-chusetts bar a year—whoops, two years—ago, I had never, for obvious reasons, actually *worked* for so much as a day as a lawyer. Naturally this filled me with massive amounts of shame, guilt, and remorse, and yet—I had to admit it, in some little corner of my psyche, I was also perversely proud. Not that I was a lawyer, but that I was throwing away something other people would have given their right arm for. One of my most cherished notions, all evidence to the contrary, was that I was . . . unique somehow. Special. A lawyer spending her mornings at JT's Place: how many people could say they'd had *that* experience? In my saner moments I realized this *was* unique, though perhaps not something of which to be proud.

Head pounding, I sat up, got my feet on the floor, and with some difficulty made my way to the "desk"—a plate-glass window stolen from a construction site balanced on two

stacks of milk crates. Overflowing ashtrays, beetle-black ro-
tary phone half-buried under old newspapers, and–oh praise
be, oh thank you, thank you, a million times thank you–not
one but two half glasses of flat, stale, warm beer. I brought
one back to bed, pulled the mangy blanket up to my chin,
and took a sip. God knew I needed a bracer, for the truly
gruesome time was upon me now, the time of reckoning that
occurred each morning: the time when I attempted to piece
together what had happened the night before.

Apparently there'd been people up here; there were
Camels and Kools stamped out on the saucer I was using, a
roach on the dresser. Plus I would never have brought beer
home myself: I always stayed at the bars till last call, and the
stores were always closed by then; plus I was too cheap and
had no foresight, especially at that hour. So at any rate, okay,
let's see . . . I'd taken a cab to Misty's . . . Kieran was tending
bar . . . Dot was there . . . Patrick had bought us a couple of
rounds . . . Tony . . . I stopped dead, cigarette, halfway to
mouth, in hand. A bloodcurdling memory had suddenly
dredged itself up from my subconscious: I had made out with
Tony. I had *made out with fucking Tony at the bar.* Oh God. Oh
no. Tony not only had an abysmally low IQ, he was also
friends with Kieran, whom I had a huge crush on and who,
even though he wasn't in the least bit interested in me, would
know I was a total whore (like he didn't already, as I'd already slept with all his other friends) and be jealous. What
could I possibly have been thinking? No, I totally remembered now, it was right after I'd done those lines in the bathroom and then Dot and I had gone out back and smoked a

joint. After that, things got very fuzzy. I had a vague impression that Dot might have stayed with me till the end, but I had no idea what time I'd left, how I'd gotten home, who'd been up here, and how long he, she, or they had stayed. Another night, added to the hundreds that had gone before, shrouded in mystery. Really, when you thought about it, it was creepy. My own life was a secret to me.

God did I feel like shit, I thought, sinking facedown in despair and pulling the blankets over my head like a shroud. I probably needed at the very least a blood transfusion and probably several I.V. lines of vitamins, liquids, and nutrients. I could hardly believe I had to work, never mind come home afterward, get dressed, and go up to New Hampshire to see my family. I counted backward from ten, willed myself to spring up, catapulted myself back to the desk, and dialed the operator to see what time it was: oh Jesus, nine-twenty, I *had* to get my ass in gear. I dragged myself down the hall to the shower, dragged myself back, yanked my dirty uniform out of the plastic bag into which I'd stuffed it before hitting the bars, gave it a shake, and pulled it on: a rayon dress of dark brown and white that smelled like week-old French fries. A spray of Chamade under each pit—in spite of everything, for some reason I always had good perfume—a comb through my wet hair, and I was ready. I took a quick look in the mirror: oh hideous, *hideous!* Why was I so *ugly?* And *fat?* No wonder nobody ever wanted me. Book for the subway, check; meager stash of money, check; key, check. I padlocked the door behind me.

There was no easy way to get to Sam's: you had to take

the Green Line to the Red Line, and even from there it was a walk. Out on the street, I headed down the gloom of Causeway toward North Station, turned down Canal, and ducked into Macy's, which had a discount bin filled with stuff that was barely a cut above pruno but dirt cheap. I'd started off drinking after work, then before work, then during work: now I just drank all the time. $2.89 pint of moldy potato mash in hand, I walked across to the subway station and, on the platform, took a nip—it tasted like nail-polish remover. When the train pulled in, I found a seat and opened *The Habit of Being*: the collected letters of Flannery O'Connor. Books were the closest thing I had to God—even at my worst I still made a pilgrimage to the public library every week or so for a fresh stack—and O'Connor was my heroine, literary and otherwise. I had read her short stories so many times that some of her characters—Asbury from "The Enduring Chill," Mr. Head from "The Artificial Nigger"—were more real to me than people I had actually met, and though I could not imagine being a Catholic, or understanding the Gospels, or living like a monk on a Georgia dairy farm the way she had, her fierce faith and unwavering convictions inspired in me the utmost respect. "My subject in fiction is the action of grace in territory held largely by the devil," she had written somewhere, and though I wasn't quite sure what she'd meant, the words stirred me; struck some chord in a place deeper than I could reach.

I took another nip as the car lurched to a stop, and glanced down at a letter dated 1958: "All human nature vigorously resists grace because grace changes us and the change is painful." Grace again . . . what *was* that? . . . something that happened in stories, to other people . . . and as for change, nothing had changed for me in years. I'd come to such a low pass I'd even *prayed* during my visit to Nashville–not that it had worked. Still, I had to admire O'Connor's faith, which had sustained her through, among other things, a long siege of lupus, the painful, debilitating illness from which she had died at thirty-nine. That was one thing we had in common. She'd been sick, too.

I got off at South Station, walked down Atlantic to Northern Avenue, and turned down what struck me thus far as a sadistically long wharf. Naturally, Sam's was at the very far end of it; a few more feet and it would have been in the water. It was a family restaurant: captain's chairs, the smell of chowder, plate-glass windows with a view of the harbor. I hadn't been working there long enough to know anybody, so in the ladies' locker room I said hey to the other gals, then went into a bathroom stall with my purse and guzzled enough vodka to get me through the punch-in, the setting up of my station, and the depressing sight, as eleven o'clock neared, of the customers outside the door waiting to get in, many of whom included families with young children. I had never been crazy about children. They made me nervous and I was jealous of them somehow, probably because they got so much attention, and they were heinous to wait on: the high chair, the tray filled with chewed-up food, the crap on the rug after they left. Plus, children don't tip.

For the next four hours I hustled plates of fish-and-chips and fried clams, my hands smeared with ketchup, my shoes splashed with coffee, my head pulsing cruelly, as if protesting the residue of nicotine, stale vodka, and tormented sleep deprivation that coursed through every vein. The manager walked by at one point, snapping his fingers at me as if I were a coolie, and when I snuck out back for a cigarette around two, the dishwashers, out for their own smoke, gave me a dirty look, got up en masse from their perch near the Dumpsters, and moved. It was a beautiful fall day, the sun sparkling on the whitecaps, but to say nature had ceased to move me would have been something of an understatement. Somewhere, in another world, gay groups of people were driving through the mountains exclaiming at the autumn foliage, planning meals together, having babies. *I am so tired*, I thought as I wedged the last of my Winston between the slats of the wharf and pushed it into the oily water below, *I am so, so tired*. Waves splashed forlornly against the barnacled pilings, and the beaks of the seagulls, tearing off pieces of rotting fish, were a deep buttery yellow, like yellow ivory.

Back inside, the last of the lunch crowd was straggling out. I restocked my station, punched out, walked back up the sadistically long wharf, took the Red Line to the Green Line to Haymarket and, before hitting home, stopped off at the Stone Lounge. Sitting in a corner sipping Miller Lites—an occasional calorie-counting measure designed to counteract the effects of decades of no exercise and a daily booze intake equivalent to several meals—I smoked, brooded, and tried to garner my strength for the night ahead. Auden's "Musée des Beaux Arts" drifted to mind: "About suffering they were never wrong, / The Old Masters . . ." Dimly realizing I was withstanding a degree of pain normal people didn't–or wouldn't–suffering was a subject I contemplated frequently. Was I being groomed for some special mission? What possible purpose could an existence like mine serve? When I wasn't drinking in crappy bars, I was home by myself reading: a life that was achingly lonely, and yet perversely designed to prevent anybody from ever getting close enough to really know me. Then again, I hardly knew myself, and the thought of having to take a good, hard look was one of the main reasons I'd stayed lost in an alcoholic daze for the last twenty years. Sin is the failure to grow, I'd read somewhere. If that were true, I thought as I stood up to leave and threw down a few bucks for the bartender, I'd been in a state of sin since I was thirteen.

No time to worry about that now, though; I had to go home and get ready for tonight. I passed the Government Square parking garage, scurried across the entrance to the Southeast Expressway, and hustled down Merrimac Street. On the curb in front of 121, some of my neighbors were passing around a pint and comparing lotto tickets. Upstairs, I hauled an old bag of ice out of the freezer, banged it against the floorboards till a chunk broke off, threw it in a beer mug with what was left of my vodka, changed into my one decent pair of jeans, and put on my favorite Dolly Parton album. I'd always had one foot in this world and one foot in a fantasy world, plus my heart had been hemorrhaging blood since the day I'd discovered boys, so country and western was right up my alley: a source of comfort, relief, camaraderie. Late at night I often stood in front of the mirror and pretended I was

Patsy Cline, and as Dolly segued into one of my favorites—
"It's All Wrong, but It's All Right"—I lit another cigarette and
took a huge swallow, letting the vodka slide voluptuously
down my throat. For a minute the old familiar feeling—life,
light, hope—returned. Everything *was* all right—or would be
soon. Everyone hits a bad patch now and again.

By the time Dan pulled up outside, honking his horn, I'd
reached the semi-anesthetized "life of the party" state I'd been
aiming for since that morning. "Be right down," I yelled out
the window, and poured the rest of my drink into a plastic
travel mug for the ride. I took the four flights at a sprint, ice
cubes sloshing. Just as I reached the door, I stopped dead in
my tracks.

Oh *fuck*, I thought. I'd forgotten to buy my father a present.

one

That you may be justified when you give
  sentence
and be without reproach when you judge.
O see, in guilt I was born,
a sinner I was conceived.

—Psalm 51

Perhaps it's true that geography is destiny, for the distinguishing feature of my New Hampshire childhood was the gigantic hole behind our house known simply as "the Pit." My older brother and sister set off cherry bombs in the Pit, we staged snowball battles in the Pit, the view from my bedroom window was of the Pit: a big, gouged-out pit, with bare, dun-brown runnels and washes that had been excavated to provide gravel for Route 95, the interstate turnpike that ran a mile west of our backyard. Chin mashed to the sill, I gazed out over that unsightly gash, burning it into my brain as a metaphor for the dry well I somehow already knew I was fated to spend my life trying to fill.

In 1958, the year I started first grade, my father built the house we lived in: a brick-and-shingle four-bedroom garrison with a double garage and a breezeway. I once heard a woman say that when God gave her something she had prayed for, He usually attached to it a condition that somehow also made it as if she *hadn't* gotten what she prayed for. Now I see it wasn't God so much as my own compulsively negative thinking, but I knew exactly what she meant, for while our house was sturdy, well-maintained, and clean, all I could see were its defects, its faults, the things it lacked. In the shower, a cheap plastic accordion door jumped its runners every time it was opened or closed. The storm windows, booby-trapped with broken catches, crashed down like dumbbells on defenseless fingers. The landscaping comprised a mangy bed of myrtle, a patchy lawn—"dry as a coco mat," my father mourned each August—and a crab-apple tree that defied every law of nature by staying the exact same size for the next forty years.

In summer, Dad kept a vegetable garden, but he had no truck with heirloom tomatoes, herbs, gay patches of marigolds. He grew cabbages, carrots, potatoes, as if we were Russian peasants storing up for a winter on the steppe—which wasn't that far off the mark. Every so often a blast shattered the air over breakfast; the old man would lean out of the upstairs bathroom window with his .22. "Got the bastard!" he'd cry in triumph, and I'd look out beyond my plate of pancakes to see a small brown woodchuck crumpling to the ground among the beet plants.

*   *   *

Born with a black cloud over my head, every tiny thing a struggle, I was tormented from the start by the skewed perspective and overwrought nerves that would later make oblivion so inviting. I looked well-adjusted enough on the outside, but on the inside, my distorted thoughts had already begun to double back, settle into obsessive ruts, feed on themselves. Telltale signs of a prematurely twisted psyche—morbid sensitivity, exaggerated fear—leaked out all over the place, just as an apparently healthy gum, in the early stages of pyorrhea, when pressed sometimes oozes blood.

Those were the days of Sputnik, Khrushchev, the Iron Curtain; of air-raid drills when our teacher, Mrs. Strout, would instruct us to put our hands over our ears and—in the ever-so-slightly doomed hope that a laminated slab of wood and four metal legs would prevent us from being incinerated by an atom bomb—crawl beneath our desks. They were also the days of TV shows with names such as *The Twilight Zone* and *The Outer Limits*; shows whose central paradigm was the existential dilemma; shows featuring men in suits with terrified eyes and sweat above their upper lips, women in shirtwaists fleeing in panic from Empire State Building–sized gorillas, Martians, mutant blobs.

I, too, was seized with panic: watching those shows, I was convinced they would get us, they would chase us down, they would stick needles in us and take us away on their spaceships. I didn't know that the enemy was not outside, but within. I didn't know that the enemy had been creeping through the family of mankind, in one way or another, since

Eve succumbed to the serpent. I didn't know that the enemy was me.

Mom and Dad couldn't afford extravagances like amusement parks or bowling alleys, but the July after second grade, a bus filled with other nature-bound grade-schoolers stopped in front of our house each morning, picked me up, and drove us to Camp Gundalow. For a summer here and there, for a month at least, we all got to go to day camp, but with my two closest-in-age siblings seven years older and five years younger than me, that year I went alone. Camp Gundalow was on the outskirts of Greenland, the adjacent town, and, with its relatively free-form schedule, its shadowed clearings where we learned to send smoke signals in case we got lost, the hushed trails that Indians had once trod, was far removed, it seemed to me, from everyday time and space. The lodge was hung with hand-lettered displays—drooping snake skins, one-winged moths; the mess hall smelled of warm pine and dust. In the mornings, we identified wildflowers and pinned beetles to corkboard; afternoons, we wove lanyards out of gimp and made Popsicle-stick cuff-link caddies. At four o'clock, before the bus came to take us home again, the flag was lowered and folded: a camper at each end—halves, halves again, triangle, ends folded under.

I, too, wanted to be a good citizen, but one part of camp resisted my allegiance—the swimming pool: ice blue, smelling of chlorine and rubber. I couldn't relax into the rhythm, couldn't let go; didn't trust the bleachy water not to flood into my nose and mouth and lungs, to reach out and take me under, like one of those mutant TV aliens. While the other kids did jack-knives and cannonballs, I struggled along the shallow end: arms stiff and unyielding, hands rigid, self-conscious claws. My campmates progressed through to Porpoise and even Whale. I barely made it from Tadpole to Minnow.

The last day of camp was Field Day. That morning I signed up for the two-legged race, the potato-sack run, and the broad jump, and then, with the same longing for redemption that impels a sinning supplicant to the altar, wandered over to the swimming pool. A mimeographed sheet listed the events: the butterfly, the crawl relay, the breath hold. The breath hold?! My heart leaped. Here, at last, was a water activity at which it might be possible to excel.

I signed my name with shaky fingers, obsessed about it all through the other, less emotionally fraught events, and, terrified they'd start without me, showed up at the pool fifteen minutes early. The others—tan, confident—performed casual practice dives and joked with Jeff, the fifteen-year-old counselor whose bare chest and thrilling underarm hair radiated a godlike unapproachability. I hung back in the shadows, nervously wondering whether we were supposed to bunch together or spread out, whether I'd be better off in the shallow or the deep end, whether you were allowed to hold on to the edge or had to tread water.

"Take your places," Jeff hollered. I found a spot near the middle and gingerly lowered myself in. "One, two, three, *under!*" I gulped air, held my nose, and ducked. *One, one thousand, two, one thousand*... The pink skirt of last year's bathing suit fluttered gently. *Twenty-two, one thousand, twenty-three, one thousand*... Silvery water bubbles floated on the surface of my undernourished thighs. *Thirty-eight, one thousand, thirty-nine, one thousand*... The whistle blew once, and then again and again as the others gave up and shot through the surface of the water. When I finally came up myself, purple and gasping, I was on the verge of requiring CPR, but I had done it: I had won first place in the breath hold.

"Atta girl," Jeff said as he began setting up for the ring toss, and Charlene, a seventh-grader so developed she already wore a bra, absentmindedly patted my arm as she walked by.

It lasted only a minute, but already I was willing to go to any lengths for a drop of approval, a dribble of a sense of belonging, a trickle of the feeling that I was loved. Already I was practically willing to die for it.

two

I will lead the blind on their journey;
by paths unknown I will guide them.
I will turn darkness into light before them,
and make crooked ways straight.

— Isaiah 42:10–16

Families with alcoholism are known for keeping secrets,
but mine took the concept to new heights. It wasn't until
I was in third grade that the mystery of my brother Skip
(eight years older than me; a wise guy), and sister Jeanne
(seven years older; boy-crazy), was cleared up. I'd always felt
a difference between us, more than could be accounted for by
just the gap in our ages, and though they'd started slipping
the words "half brother" and "half sister" into our conversations, I had no idea what those terms meant. "Mom's not our
real mother, Mom's not our real mother," they'd begun taunt-
ing as we fought over the household comb, or threw rolled-up
pellets of sponge-like twenty-five-cents-a-loaf Bonnie Maid

bread at each other, but I figured they were just jerking me around as usual. If it was something I was supposed to know, wouldn't Mom have explained it? The only other person in the family at the time was Joe, my baby brother, but at three obviously *he* didn't know. Where did babies come from, anyway? I wondered uneasily.

Mom's natural reserve discouraged prying, and it was a cold, windy March day when I finally gathered the courage to broach the subject. We were in the backyard at the clothesline, bundled up in parkas and taking down a row of underpants that had frozen as stiff and hard as if they'd been dipped in plaster of Paris.

"Skip and Jeanne say you're not really their mother," I said, lips clenched to protect my already overly sensitive teeth from the cold. "What does that mean?"

The clothespin she'd been holding clattered to the frozen ground, and I knew I'd strayed into forbidden territory. There was a long pause while she gazed across the scrub-stubbled snow and into a stand of leafless elms. Her clear blue eyes had a set but pitying look to them, as if the time had come to tell me I'd been sired by an ax murderer.

"Dad was . . . well, he was . . . married before," she whispered hoarsely. "He's . . . he's *divorced.*"

A hundred questions rose to mind—Was the first lady pretty? Where does she live now?—but from the stricken expression on my mother's face, I instinctively knew not to press further. With a razor-like wind slicing down the backs of our necks, we knocked the ice off the rest of the clothes—

darned wool socks, patched handkerchiefs—and folded them
into the frost-rimmed wash basket in silence.

At dinner that night, I studied Skip and Jeanne closely.
They looked the same—Jeanne insisting, "All the *other* girls are
allowed to use Nair!"; Skip exclaiming, "He's a Mongoloid!
How would you like to have a driver's ed. teacher who's a
complete *Mongoloid?*"—but the fact that, along with my
beloved father, they had had a hidden life before this one;
that Mom, Dad, Skip, and Jeanne had known about it but not
me, made me feel shunted aside and invisible. My parents
had always been vague about the specifics of where, when,
and how they had met. Now I interpreted this to mean that
the circumstances surrounding the birth of me—their first
child, it turned out—were too embarrassing to mention in po-
lite society, that Mom's averted eyes and hushed voice meant
that there was something unseemly and mortifying about the
way we'd begun. Why hadn't she told me before? I wondered. Were there other things I didn't know? One thing was
obvious: divorce must be a shameful, shameful thing.

Mom was as faithful and true as they come, but one thing
you were in no danger of getting on her watch was a big
head. The one time I dared to ask if I was pretty, she stole a
line from Thornton Wilder's *Our Town* and replied with an
enigmatic little smile, "Pretty enough for all practical pur-
poses." Another afternoon I came home and announced I'd
scored across-the-board 99s—out of a possible 100—on the
Iowa Test of Basic Skills, a standardized exam that, according

to the teacher, was administered to children *all over the country*. "That's nice," Mom replied blandly. "Time to set the table." When I won the school spelling bee in fifth grade, beating out kids who were three years ahead of me, I thought a small congratulations might at last be in order. Instead, Mom, who had loyally—or so I thought—come to watch, insisted I'd missed the winning word, got on the horn, and tried to badger the principal into holding a rematch.

Mom's housekeeping habits were all of a piece with her moral code: she was determined, thorough, and extremely clean. She beat away ceiling cobwebs with a sheet-wrapped broom, scrubbed the hard-to-get floor space beneath the radiators till it shone, attacked windows with crumpled-up newspaper dipped in ammonia and rubbed them so clear it's a wonder we didn't walk through them. At the end of a hard day, she liked to curl up with a bowl of popcorn and read or watch a nature show, but she would have sooner stolen than done something frivolous like complain, or go to bed without doing the dishes, or dole out spontaneous hugs.

Gearing up to be a lackadaisical housekeeper and a champion complainer myself, I was slightly cowed by all this. It wasn't that she made me feel second-rate for failing to meet her standards, it was that I already felt so second-rate myself I was afraid my myriad deficiencies would lead her to discount me altogether. My emotions were all on the surface, but Mom was the still-waters-run-deep type, and it threw me off that I never quite knew what she was thinking. Though she did all kinds of warm, motherly things—bought me books, sewed badges to my Brownie uniform, showed me a secret

place in the woods where the lady's slippers grew—I tended to
see them as flukes, not signs of devotion, and it probably
didn't help that situations of urgent concern to me often
seemed to barely enter her consciousness. When I begged for
the pair of black patent leather shoes like all the other girls
wore to school, the ones with a little strap across the instep,
Mom presented me with a pair of stout boy's oxfords, saying
firmly, "There. Now your feet won't splay." When Jeanne
yelled down that the upstairs bathroom was on fire—and I
panicked that we'd all be burned to cinders—Mom tranquilly
finished playing "Onward, Christian Soldiers" on the piano
before going to investigate. Every family trip began the same
way: shit-brown Vista Cruiser station wagon loaded, tank
full, Dad sitting in the driver's seat, map at the ready, fuming,
while inside Mom dialed up one more member of her Bible
group, or decided that now was the time to get out the ironing board, fill the sprinkler bottle, and apply a little elbow
grease to the blouse she planned on wearing that day.

"Most people are descended from the apes," Dad would
tell us, checking his watch for the hundredth time. "Mother's
family came down from mules!"

Why didn't she try to make him happy? I wondered anxiously. Didn't she care about making things *right*?

One reason my mother may not have cared quite as much as
I did about making things right was that she was just a tad
busy around that time having *other* children who needed her
attention. Five years after me there'd been Joe, two years after
that would come Geordie, and a year after that, Dan. (Mere-

dith, the baby, was born later, when I was a freshman in high school.) Mom tried to enlist my aid, but lacking the maternal instinct, I wasn't much help. While she was preoccupied with cooking, changing diapers, and doing laundry, I made it my job to focus, with my tuned-to-dysfunction radar, on signs of the kind of emotional imbalance I already recognized all too well in myself. "Joe's mental," I'd report as he sat in the corner ritualistically putting on and taking off his little sneakers, or, "Joe's depressed," as he banged his tiny head against the wall.

"Could you *please* go sweep the floor?" Mom would ask, and I'd flounce off, fantasizing about the day when I'd grow up and enter the *real* world, and people would *finally* appreciate me.

Someone had to support this growing tribe: that person was my father, whose life was dominated by the mythic struggle known as "work." Every morning, he went off with his battered red-and-white Igloo cooler, and every night he came home staggering with exhaustion: his thermos drained of instant lemonade, his baloney sandwich reduced to a crumb or two buried in a crumpled piece of wax paper. "Jesus, was it hot today!" he moaned in summer, collapsing against the fake-wood Formica kitchen counter and, in winter, "*Bitter* cold. Bitter!"

Dad was a bricklayer, but he didn't have the burly, muscle-bound physique of his construction-worker friends. He was a modest figure, in his long-sleeved blue chambray work shirt and Sears jeans, and his thin shoulders seemed hardly strong enough to carry the burden of his ever-expanding family.

Emotionally, he wasn't a stereotypical construction worker, either. Every fall, he planted an amaryllis bulb in a plastic pot, set it in the dining-room window, and marveled over its progress till it bloomed. He recited poetry: Housman's "When I was one-and-twenty . . ."; Masefield's "I must go down to the seas again, to the lonely sea and the sky . . ." He had the twin Irish traits of melancholy and charm, a soft spot for the underdog–welfare mothers, Little League pitchers with leukemia–and, to hide his emotions, a black black sense of humor. For a while we all watched *Lassie* together, partly to make fun of it and partly because we ached for that kind of closeness ourselves. "What, is he planning on opening a flower shop?" Dad snickered as Timmie ran through a field of daisies with his faithful dog. At the end of the show, I looked over and he was wiping away tears. "Must have gotten something in my eye," he said with a little smirk.

Dad saw the world as a place of mystery and beauty, but it gnawed at him that things could go so consistently, abysmally wrong, and in a world fraught with danger, his way of protecting us was an almost insane overabundance of caution. "The Floyds invited me to the lake," I announced. "Remember that Kelleher boy who pitched over the side of a canoe and drowned?" Dad mused. "Can I learn how to ski?" Joe begged. "Was it last year that girl from Epping wandered off the trail and froze to death?" Dad replied. "For Crimey's sake!" he railed in the parking lots of grocery stores, spotting a cart left by a careless shopper. "If that thing ever got rolling, it could pick up momentum, barrel right into a three- or four-year-old kid . . ." He shook his head, leaving us to imagine the twitching limbs, the crushed skull bleeding onto the asphalt.

Convinced at any given time that we were headed for the poorhouse, however, his biggest obsession was money. Over dinner I watched as, lips moving, he sketched numbers in the air above the table, my own brow anxiously furrowing along with his as he mentally balanced the pitiless scales of need: Skip's football uniform against Jeanne's prom dress, new shoes for me against a set of horseshoes for the boys. As he handed us an item that he had scrimped and saved to buy—a toy saw, a communal scooter—his face was a study in conflicts: hope versus fear, giving versus holding on, the pleasure of the moment lost as his mind fast-forwarded from the shiny packaging, the smell of fresh varnish or new rubber, to the inevitable day when we would break it, lose it, hurt ourselves with it.

Mom was an enigma whose depths I couldn't hope to plumb, but my father, whose anxiety I had inherited down to my marrow, I understood completely. Every time one of us dropped a bottle of milk, broke a window, lost a pair of pliers, I saw it through his eyes: not a run-of-the-mill mistake but a doomsday omen, a sign that the family was headed for disaster. That was how to help out, I thought to myself. I could not take up too much room. I could not take foolish risks. I could never ever make a mistake myself.

three
_____

Love in practice is a hard and dreadful thing
compared to love in dreams.

—Fyodor Dostoyevsky

M y parents were welcoming hosts, giving neighbors, and generous to a fault, but even an objective observer might have noted the bare-bones approach to material goods that permeated every aspect of our household. The Band-Aid box contained only one Band-Aid, the minuscule size meant for shaving nicks. The Bactine bottle was perpetually empty save for the dram trapped in the nozzle. Shoe polish had to be gouged from the sides of the tin with a toothpick. Like Communists, we enjoyed no private ownership: there was one hula hoop, one basketball, one sled.

Heat was likewise in woefully short supply. From October through April we slept between sheets that felt as if they'd been stored in a refrigerator, and dressed each morning in rooms so cold they could have doubled as meat lockers. Shivering before the bathroom sink, we took twice-a-week sponge baths (showers wasted water), scrubbing ourselves with washcloths that, hung out on the wind-whipped clothesline, had dried as stiff and rough as sandpaper. Partly this was to save on oil, and partly it was because my mother had the metabolism of a penguin and liked nothing better than to throw the windows open mid-winter, strip down to her shirtsleeves, and catch a frigid Arctic breeze. As blizzards raged and the wind hurled in from the east, I crept about the house swathed in sweaters, my lips blue. "For heaven's sake, don't you want some fresh air?" she'd exclaim, throwing open the front door to admit a gust of icy snow.

When it came to food, the portions were mingy and angst-producing: a thimbleful of coleslaw apiece, five hot dogs for seven people (were we supposed to be learning fractions? I wondered). Like a plague of locusts, we laid the table bare: a chicken reduced to a pile of dry bones, corn cobs stripped of kernels. Fights broke out over the last meatball or pork chop, the combatants hollow-eyed and clawing, the victor holding aloft a lopsided baking-soda biscuit as if it were a haunch of beef. Mom bought sale items in bulk (always ones I detested even singly): twenty cans of lima beans, a gross of stewed tomatoes. In the fall, we drove with Dad to Applecrest for "drops"—fruit that had fallen off the tree and partially rotted.

I understood it was no mean feat to support so many people, and now I know it wasn't so much the events of my childhood that shaped me as my reaction to them. Still, predisposed as I was to view even neutral situations through the lens of hyperbolic paranoia, this chronic deprivation had a peculiarly acute effect on me. It gave rise to a scarcity mentality where there was only one of everything—choice, chance, group of friends; to belief in a universe that was anything but welcoming, anything but abundant, anything but accommodating. I could have looked at our household as proof that God provided; instead I was in a constant panic that what little we had would run out. I could have trusted in my parents' continued competence; instead I lived in terror of their imminent physical and emotional collapse.

Living in a big family could have taught me to share. Instead, I became a hoarder, secreting away whatever I could scrounge: money, food, feelings. Other girls read biographies of Amelia Earhart or Eleanor Roosevelt. My heroine was Hetty Green, billed in *Guinness World Records* as the stingiest woman on earth. Though she'd squirreled away millions of dollars, Hetty ate cold oatmeal for breakfast, wore the same black dress every day, and had a son whose leg had been amputated because she was too cheap to pay a doctor. Stockpiling against future want was an idea written deep in my bones and blood, and without yet fully knowing why, I thrilled in homage to the person who had brought it to such pathological lengths. It was the same idea that, years later, would compel me to have a few martinis not because I wasn't feeling good then, but in case I might not be feeling good in an hour; to "brace up" with a pint or so of gin *before* going to the bar; to order, already falling-down drunk, three more scotches at last call. You had to store up! You had to stave off disaster! You could never, ever have enough.

*   *   *

Someone with a firmer grip on reality might have regarded my incessantly toiling mother and father and concluded that they were in charge, but throughout my entire childhood I labored under the illusion that my family's well-being depended solely on *me*. One reason for this was that by the time I was nine, Skip and Jeanne had moved out, leaving me the functionally oldest child. The other reason was that I was smart. Not just run-of-the-mill smart, but the smartest kid in class, a straight-A student until I was in eleventh grade (when I got my first B-plus and the world as I knew it ended). Even as a child I realized this was a gift, and even as a child I realized that, like most gifts, it was a mixed blessing. It made me feel special, but it also made me feel more alone. It made me feel proud, but it also gave me an overdeveloped sense of guilt and responsibility. Mom was smart, but she'd dropped out of college to start having us. Dad was smart, but not school smart like me. I was the one whose smartness would wipe out this blight, would redeem us in the eyes of the world. It was up to me to save the family from shame.

108 Post Road was half my universe. The other half lay three miles east on Atlantic Avenue: North Hampton Elementary, a drab two-story brick building with a statue of Paul Revere in front, a playground in back, and halls smelling of sour milk, dirty socks, and wet paper towels.

I was good at everything. In history I knew the biographies of Florence Nightingale, Eli Whitney, and Nathan Hale. In math I memorized my multiplication tables up to nine, mastered long division, and was starting to grasp decimals. In geography I created my first and only piece of conceptual art by tracing a map of Brazil from the encyclopedia, coating it with Elmer's glue and sprinkling on a layer of coffee grounds. Still, I had grasped since Day One that what I was really learning was to loathe my haircut, my clothes, the very food I ate—which is why the real reason I went to school was reading. From the moment I'd learned how letters coalesce into words, I knew I'd tapped into a parallel world—a reward for the misery of living in this one—and I'd been devouring stories, poems, fairy tales, Nancy Drew mysteries, comics, dictionaries, bird guides, and the backs of cereal boxes with rapturous devotion ever since. In class, my hand was always waving obnoxiously in the air—Call on me! Call on me! I screamed inwardly. For show-and-tell I brought in my most precious possession, a book called *The Illustrated Treasury of Children's Literature*, displaying it to the class as reverently as if it were a copy of the Gutenberg Bible. And just crossing the threshold of the school library gave me a jolt I realized only years later was clearly sexual. I dreamily perused the shelves, snuck clandestine sniffs of the ink pad, and presented my manila cards to the librarian to be stamped with the swoony intoxication of a besotted inamorata.

I loved the way books looked, loved the way books smelled, loved that books made me forget. My favorites were *The Diary of Anne Frank*, *The Yearling*, *Uncle Tom's Cabin*: tales of grotesque cruelty and unbearable loss. That was precisely why I liked them. Even back then I understood the real purpose of literature. I didn't want to hear that people lived happily ever after. I wanted to know that other people suffered, too.

four

Fear not, my children; call out to God.
He who has brought this upon you will
   remember you.

—Baruch 4:21

If there was one trait prized above all others in our household, it was the ability to withstand and hide emotional and physical pain. Any attempt to communicate one's feelings–grief, hurt–was viewed as unseemly melodrama; any show of disappointment–that, say, you'd *told* her you liked the blue dress better so why had she gone and bought the pink one?–as hysterical self-indulgence; and when my father crushed his finger in a vise one weekend, we all understood it was far better that he'd driven himself to the hospital, blood spurting, rather than to have "bothered" a friend.

When it came to sibling dynamics, this meant we had one basic mode of communication–ridicule; and one basic mode of interaction–violence. It wasn't that we didn't love one another; it was just that we showed our affection in ways that might have seemed strange to an outsider who didn't realize we were only toughening up one another for the even greater cruelties that lay beyond our walls. When we weren't slapping, punching, stabbing, pushing, throwing rocks, or flicking wet towels at one another, we played Pig Pile (adopted from the Salem witch trials), snuck Tabasco into one another's milk, and administered the elbow treatment, a potentially fatal maneuver that consisted of pinning the victim to the floor and grinding an elbow into the softest part of the temple until he or she screamed for mercy.

Most of our (I say "our," but since I was the oldest and therefore instigated most of it, "my" would be more accurate) torture, however, was psychological. One of my favorite tricks was selecting a despised nickname and chanting it at the person until he was on the verge of a psychotic break. For my scrawny brother Dan: Boney; Green Teeth; Chief Blackfoot—because he wouldn't take a bath. Geordie was known as Eva, after a hapless classmate who'd sent him a Valentine's Day card and who I forever after insisted had a crush on him. Joe, because he pouted, I named Lip. "Li-ip, Li-ip," we all taunted in maddening, sing-songy voices. And we all called one another "queer"—not as in gay, but as in uncool or weak or allowing oneself to be vulnerable in any way. Childlike happiness was queer, caring too much was queer, and the expression of any feeling other than self-pity or contempt was queer squared. The slightest sign of emotion in even our most beloved TV characters was treated with the same warm concern we reserved for one another. "Haw, haw, haw, look,

Heath, Opie's bawlin'." "Check it out, Heath, the Beav's all mad at Wally, what a queer."

In those long-ago days, we had no computer games to absorb us. We held fight-to-the-death Ping-Pong tournaments in the cellar, crashing into the woodstove as we lunged for returns; hurling the paddle at our opponent's face or groin if he or she made a bad call. We played baseball in the vacant lot across the street, our knuckles swollen from catching line drives with our bare hands. In winter we went "sliding." Sliding in our neighborhood was nothing like those Currier & Ives illustrations of red-cheeked children merrily sailing down a soft, snow-heaped slope. It was a bone-rattling, death-defying suicide mission down a wall of sheer ice pocked with bumps, sharp-edged stones, and frozen reeds that lashed our faces like whips. Four-year-olds went out in wind-chill factors of thirty below dressed in thin rubber boots lined with plastic bread wrappers; and only the sheerest luck saved at least one of us from suffering frostbite, a severed spine, or permanent brain trauma.

Though we used the gentlest slope, we were able to work up a surprising amount of speed, and within minutes all exposed flesh—foreheads, inner wrists between the shrunken mittens and the too short sleeves of the hand-me-down coats—would be lacerated and bleeding from where we'd been dumped and broken through crusts of frozen snow. The next most dangerous vehicle—inevitably missing a slat or sporting a broken rudder—was the Flexible Flyer. Sissies rode sitting up; the rest of us threw ourselves on belly-first and barreled down at top speed. Here the danger was being blinded by stinging blackberry vines, colliding with the to-boggan, or—since we often took off from a steeper slope that was perpendicular to and intersected the gentler slope before continuing on, making for a hair-raising interlude when one was temporarily airborne—breaking a rib.

For a truly maniacal ride, however, nothing beat the flying saucer, a shallow aluminum bowl—just big enough to accom-modate a child sitting cross-legged—that was incapable of be-ing steered. The full effect required taking off from a bony, almost vertical precipice that, due to the fact that we were the only ones in the neighborhood insane enough to use it, had not been even minimally denuded of bramble bushes, giant rocks, and copses of medium-sized trees. In what should by all rights have been the last moments before one of us suc-cumbed to quadriplegia, here at last we displayed a grudging affection. "Geor-*die!*" we'd cheer in admiration as he went shooting sideways down the hill, bashed his tailbone on a boulder, bounced four feet into the air, and, frantically trying to break his fall, came down with the force of a sledgehammer on one or both hands.

Mom waved off our pleas for medical treatment in such situations with a chuckle. One day I came in from the Pit with my left hand dangling from my wrist like the broken neck of a lamb.

"It's killing me, Mom!" I wailed, cradling it against my chest. "I think I broke it."

"Come now," she smiled briskly. "Let's not whine."

"Mom! I'm not kidding. I have to go to the doctor right away!"

"Nonsense," she replied and, grabbing hold of the offending hand, deftly wrenched the bone back into place.

Never one to pamper, Mom believed in warm washcloths in place of casts, ginger ale in place of morphine, and salt water in place of antibiotics, penicillin, and periodontal surgery. When Danny got appendicitis, I could almost see her mentally weighing the alternatives: an expensive hospital, or a darning needle and a length of catgut? My father had had all his teeth pulled when he was twenty-nine, and I always got the impression that my mother didn't think dentures—how much could a jumbo box of generic Polident have cost?—were a bad idea for all of us.

It was small wonder that I, for one, had cavity-prone teeth. Every chance I got, I begged, borrowed, or stole some change and rode my bike past the Joneses (natives) and the Coles (carpetbaggers from Massachusetts), then sailed smoothly down the hill, past the intersection with Exeter Road, the Corlisses (down-home vegetable stand in summer: eight wormy tomatoes, a dented but delicious peach pie)—and on to what was officially called the Post Road Grocery but we referred to as the Little Store, a white-painted cottage with flower boxes at the windows and a couple of gas pumps out front that looked innocuous enough, but was actually the childhood equivalent of a crack house.

Inside, the cadaverous Mr. Lembeck tended the till, and though there were also shelves of groceries, racks of nuts, and a hot-dog steamer, I had eyes only for the candy. Wax fangs, fireballs, Bonomo's Turkish Taffy that attracted fillings like magnets. Caramel, licorice, marshmallow, chocolate; Creamsicles, Fudgsicles, Eskimo pies. Root beer and Fanta Orange. Devil Dogs, Twinkies, coconut-covered Hostess Sno Balls. Outside on the picnic table I laid out my score like a junkie and fixed on the uplifting rush of raw sugar.

When your cosmos consists of a few square miles, every landmark assumes archetypal significance. The Pit was the depressing place, school was the proving-ground place, the library was the idyllic place. But in a class by itself, I saw already, was the Little Store. That was the place you went to get relief.

five

On their banks dwell the birds of heaven;
from the branches they sing their song.
                                    —Psalm 104

Books, fantasy, sugar . . . now I discovered yet another new drug: hermitdom. I hadn't yet heard those stories of the desert fathers who balanced on pillars for fourteen years or let their beards grow and lived in caves, but if I had, I would have been green with envy.

I wanted to be alone partly because my own world was so absorbing that other people's seemed invasive and bothersome, partly because even back then my self-sabotaging solution to loneliness was to isolate even more, and partly because I swear I was a child contemplative. St. John of the Cross, writing *Dark Night* in his prison turret, had nothing on me. I spent hours alone in my bedroom—a spare, cell-like enclosure featuring a plain maple bureau and a single twin bed—

yelling at anyone who ventured by to go away, bitterly protesting when my mother interrupted to ask me to wash dishes or babysit: staring into space, brooding, trying to figure out how the world worked. Why was there something instead of nothing? Why was I here and not there? One night, scrunched up on the floor trying to get warm, I discovered that by pressing my head tightly to my knees I could enter an almost trancelike state: a combination of sensory deprivation, blood rushing to my head, and a genuine, if accidental, emptying of the mind, which I had no idea at the time is the aim of all deep meditation and prayer.

I did not connect this feeling in any way with God. I did, of course, *believe* in God—judgment, eternal damnation: these were ideas that came easily to me. My idea of how He operated was pretty much based on New England weather: three months of paradise, nine of hell—I could do the math. Winter was obviously a *punishment* for summer, a reflection of the universal law that every moment of happiness had to be paid for with three of misery.

Sunday school, which Mom shanghaied us all into attending each week, did nothing to alter this view. The kids I was starting to like had parents who smoked cigarettes and watched TV Sunday mornings, but Mom was a faithful parishioner at the Congregational church: one of those foursquare, white-steepled churches that have been the subject of a million New England postcards, it was right across the town common from our house. The outside was all too familiar: we waited on the front steps every morning, usually in the sub-tundra freezing cold, for the bus. Inside, it was almost creepily plain, with clear, unstained-glass windows, an empty cross above the altar, and the kind of stark, unforgiving light that brings to mind pillories and stocks, fire-and-brimstone-spouting preachers, and the fate of Hester Prynne.

Sunday school was the kindly but unexciting teacher Mr. Griffin, who owned a goat farm on Hobbs Road; it was parables about old men in dusty tunics; it was pictures of the Virgin Mary looking way cleaner and calmer than any mother I had ever seen as she gazed at the also weirdly calm baby Jesus. One picture in my blue clothbound Bible was of a grown-up Jesus, with wavy brown hair, wearing a long white shawl over a red robe with sparks flying out at the bottom of it. At his feet knelt a woman, her eyes stricken with the kind of perplexed pain I knew well. Underneath, it said, "She touched the hem of his garment and was healed." That fired my imagination: that a person could have so much power it flowed out from his *clothes*.

But for the most part, counting down the minutes in a dreary classroom, I just found Sunday school irrelevant. I had more serious problems: how to get my brothers and sisters to leave me alone so I could read in peace, how to keep people from noticing that we didn't have much money, how to get rid of that feeling I had almost all the time that something was *wrong*.

The donuts in the foyer afterward were okay, but obviously lost sheep and prodigal sons and the man who lay paralyzed on his mat till Jesus came along had nothing to do with me.

* * *

What seemed way closer to a God experience occurred on Sunday afternoons, when we drove up the coast to Nana and Pa's, my father's parents. The ocean was to the people of the New Hampshire seacoast what Ayer's Rock was to the Australian aborigines—inscrutable, mysterious, ever changing but always the same—and driving along it put one in a meditative frame of mind. The waves crashed in and ebbed out with magnetic regularity, tide pools teemed with crabs and sea urchins, seaweed drifted in shallow coves like mermaid's hair. Nana and Pa lived in the wealthy town of Rye, in an ivy-covered brick house with a flagstone patio out front and a screened-in porch out back. The air smelled of salt, waves crashed on the rocky sand, and, ten miles offshore, the Isles of Shoals shimmered through a dreamy mist. The lawn was strewn with gardens of iris and tiger lilies, and flowers grew all along the gravel-lined driveway, too: bachelor's buttons, bleeding hearts, spiked hollyhocks with friendly, face-shaped blooms of claret red, seashell pink, white.

Pa was nice, too, but he'd worked so hard laying brick for fifty years (beginning in Ireland) to make this lifestyle possible that he generally tottered in, hit the nearest armchair, and promptly fell asleep. It was Nana who represented the delights of paradise, and I attached myself to her with the fervor of a pilgrim throwing herself upon the Our Lady shrine at Lourdes. I fetched her hot-water bottles—she had a bad hip—so I could pilfer the pockets of her tweed skirts for peppermints. I hugged her, entwining my fingers in her diamond necklace with such alacrity it's a wonder I didn't strangle her. I parked myself beside her on the couch and rifled through her alligator pocketbook. Every time she turned around I was smearing so much rouge on my cheeks I looked like a prostitute, or shoving her bottle of Yardley smelling salts halfway up my nose for the ammonia high, or offering to count her change in an ill-disguised bid to get her to give me some money. But the main reason I loved Nana was that she gave me so much attention. "Little Butterball," she called me, even though I wasn't even fat. "Aren't ye the bright one, though," she said as I tried to work a crossword puzzle. "Look at ye, brown as a berry," she'd say, pinching my cheeks, and I was so starved for touch I wouldn't have cared if she'd used a pair of pliers.

In my memory, it is always summer in this house, Pa has just died, and I'm about eleven–right about the time when, much as I loved my family, I was also starting to want to escape from them every chance I got. Unlike many of the people in my life, Nana seemed to actively enjoy having me around (which was probably why I never, even to myself, made fun of her), and I was constantly angling for an invite. I'd dial her up–GEneva 6-1150–and hint around: "What color's the ocean today, Nan?" "Hey Nan, isn't it neat when the tide comes in at night and you can hear the water rattling over those little stones?" "Come now and stay a few days," she'd respond, "we'll make up a nice bed," and when we drove up on Sunday I'd bring my pajamas, toothbrush, and books.

Nana still had a hint of a brogue–she'd come over on a boat when she was nineteen–and though I found similar backwardness mortifying in my mother, it slayed me that

Nana had no use for modern innovations such as television, store-bought bread, or packaged cereal. "Sawdust! Cardboard!" she cried over breakfast. "What do they call them now, Rice Kripsies [*sic*]? A wee bit of oatmeal is all a body needs, and a spot of prune juice to stay reg-lar." She'd assimilated just enough to have developed a liking for pizza, which she called "pizzy pie," and at lunchtime we often climbed into the big black Buick and motored down Ocean Boulevard, past Pirate's Cove Restaurant and 4 Winds Lobster, for an Americanized cheese and sausage at the Surfside. Nana's mode of driving was to accelerate in surges and, in between, come to an almost complete stop. It was impossible to drive with her for more than half a mile without wanting to throw up, which made me especially glad we spent most of our time at home.

Here she sewed; or made bread, slyly winging the moist ball of elastic dough against my cheek; or gabbed on the phone with her friends—Dorothy Clark, Florence Berry— from a secret organization she belonged to called the Daughters of the Eastern Star. And then she let me go, left me to what to this day I consider life's greatest luxuries: unstructured time and solitude. Alone, I didn't need to be self-conscious, and therefore sarcastic; alone, I had no chores, no turf to protect, no identity to forge; alone, I could break free from the stultifying confines of 108 Post Road and soar to the ethereal realm of pure spirit.

I did two things at this house. One was daydream. I wandered around the yard for hours, punch-drunk with the sky and the ocean and the flowers. I picked sun-warmed raspberries while tiny yellow butterflies fluttered around my head, trailed along lichen-covered stone walls, gazed out over the wind-riffled waves. In the shade of a blue spruce, I found a clump of lilies of the valley, and between the perfume-sweet smell and the waxy white cups and the lettuce-green leaves, I almost swooned. I wanted to eat the flowers; I wanted to *be* the flowers!

The other thing I did in this house was snoop, though I'm not sure snoop is the right word for something done not only with Nana's full knowledge but encouragement as well. I snooped through the cupboard of the black-and-white tiled bathroom: bars of Fels-Naptha soap, tins of Dr. Lyon's tooth powder; through the living-room breakfront: Wedgwood vases, ruby tumblers; through the chest in Nana's bedroom: a sterling silver tea set swaddled in chamois, shamrock-etched liqueur ponies, ivory lace tablecloths that trailed the scent of cedar.

Like one of those crazed collectors of R&B records or snowstorm paperweights, once I'd memorized the inventory, on every visit I obsessively insisted on cataloguing it anew. Every time I had to make the rounds; every time, to make sure the Roseville pitcher, the cut-glass salt cellar with the doll-sized spoon, and the porcelain saucer painted with green pagodas where Nana kept her hairpins were in their designated places. It was as if those things were anchors, however fragile, in a shipwreck-prone world, and maybe Nana felt that way, too. A poor girl from County Cork, the widow of a bricklayer: it must have been a marvel to have made it safely to shore, to have amassed so many solid objects that could be displayed and touched and treasured. She wasn't proprietary or snotty about them at all. "Go ahead, pick it up, hold it to the light," she said, handing me a Belleek teacup. "See how delicate—like an eggshell."

And so I snooped through the cellar, with its jars of pickles and preserves; I snooped through the pantry, with its twenty-pound bin of flour and bushels of apples; I snooped through the desk, with its smell of pecans and sewing-machine oil, pawing the drawers like a private detective: "What's a blotting pad for, Nana?" "Nan, did you know you had all these rubber bands?" "Oh look, Nana, here's a secret compartment full of stamps," and Nana only smiled. She never told me to cut the crap, never told me not to be so god-damn nosy. When I said, "Hey, Nana, look, a pair of antique scissors," she said, "Oh gory, I brought those over from the old country. Why don't you cut some peonies with them?"

And it occurs to me now, as I write, that those two things I did at Nana's—daydream and snoop—are pretty much what I do today for work.

Nana made delicious rolls, yeasty and faintly sweet with mo-lasses and feather-light. Big pans of rolls, one white, one oat-meal, glazed with butter and dusted with flour, two dozen sweet golden rolls that you broke apart and smeared with more butter. Every holiday, Nana's rolls: two big rectangular silver baking pans of Nana's rolls.

The Thanksgiving dinner after Nana died was the first time I ever saw my father cry. The last couple of years, she'd hardly eaten anything—a spoonful of mashed potatoes, a shred of turkey—and it was pretty depressing to look across to the place where she'd always sat and see Joe and Geordie slapping each other instead. We were all picking at the jelled cranberry salad and the farmer's cabbage, and all of a sudden there was a kind of strangled sound and I looked up to the head of the table and the old man was sitting there just nakedly sobbing.

"Dad!" someone said, and someone else said, "Daddy, what's the matter?"

"I miss my mother's rolls!" he said, tears streaming down his cheeks.

It was as if the ocean we had seen all those years from the windows of her house were filled now with love and sorrow, and, for once, nobody had a smart retort.

six

O the mind, mind has mountains; cliffs of fall
Frightful, sheer, no-man-fathomed. Hold
   them cheap
May who ne'er hung there.
                —Gerard Manley Hopkins,
                   "No Worst, There Is None"

I'd always looked to fellow misfits for friends, and perhaps it's no surprise that, even before I started drinking, I was gravitating toward those from alcoholic families. From sixth grade through the end of high school my best friend was Jill Vandevere who lived in a semi-mansion down at the beach. Jill had two older sisters—Mercedes and Rita—and all three of them called their parents by their first names. Doug, Jill's snobby CPA father, drove a red Triumph with plates that read ACCTNT. Charlotte, the mother, was a sharp dresser who smoked Tareytons and left after-school notes that actually said things like "I want that floor clean enough to eat off of,"

or "You better scrub that sink till it *shines!*" Due to her permanently foul temper, Jill and I took to calling her Crabwoman.

It was always tricky calling over there. *"Whaaaaaat?"*
Crabwoman would snarl if she picked up.

"Um, is Jill there, please?"

"Naaaooooooo." Click. Supposedly Crabwoman worked in
an insurance office in Boston, though it was almost impossible to imagine her interacting for any length of time with regular people.

The food situation (always a matter of paramount interest
to me) at Jill's was very strange: the kids and the grown-ups
had separate cabinets. The kids' was filled with SpaghettiOs
and Kraft macaroni and cheese, and Doug and Charlotte's
was filled with shrimp bisque and Pepperidge Farm cookies
and cans of cocktail nuts. Lots and lots of cocktail nuts to go
with their lots and lots of cocktails because they were both
unbelievable lushes: violent, vicious lushes. Charlotte once
bashed through Jill's bedroom door with a hockey stick,
Doug liked to dole out backhands, and one or another of the
kids was always putting in a call to Mr. Mahoney, the chief of
police, to come down and restore order. Mr. Mahoney was a
Barney Fife type who lived on the other end of town, re-
paired lawn mowers in his spare time, and was a huge alcoholic himself.

Jill was a good student and an excellent athlete, and
though she never turned out to have a problem with alcohol,
she did have a small issue with aggression. When I first met
her, she had a habit of sneaking up behind a person and
stomping down on his or her instep as hard as she could with

the heel of her Weejun: at recess people fled from her, terrified of the penny-loafer punishment. Also, to say she had a sharp tongue would have been an understatement: all the Vandeveres were sarcastic, but Jill was the champion. Once I persuaded her to stop trying to break my foot, we got along famously.

My other friend was Peter Parks, whose parents were both such terrible alcoholics that he never even invited anyone over to his house. His mother got so loaded one Thanksgiving that she tried to flush the turkey down the toilet, and his father was always nabbing Pete to go with him on liquor runs. The old man would buy a quart for when he got home, and a few nips for the ride, and before they were out of the parking lot, he would have torn the cap off the first one, downed it, and hooked the empty over the roof of the car.

"You hear the glass tinkling on the pavement," Pete reported, "and then he says 'Aaaaahhhhhhh,'" and we'd observe a moment of silence in the face of this slavering need that we both intuitively understood and sympathized with already—for Pete, of course, grew up to have a teensy problem with alcohol, too.

For someone with my penchant for hyperbole, junior high was not an easy time. A whitehead became a face full of running boils. The pores in my chin were as big as the holes in a cribbage board. My nose was so gigantic I was surprised a reporter from *The Portsmouth Herald* hadn't come over and written a story on it.

Such exaggerated self-criticism might have been merely

funny, or annoying, except that it was based on one of my deepest convictions: that I had to be perfect to be loved. Perhaps this was bound to come to a crisis: it happened near the end of eighth grade, when I was chosen as a finalist in the prestigious Oratorical Contest. The Oratorical Contest was the showpiece of the academic year, so notorious an event that, rather than being scheduled in the afternoon like other "assemblies," it took place at night so that not only teachers, students, and mothers, but also fathers, younger siblings, and even interested but unrelated onlookers could attend.

I'd selected as my topic the controversial "Should Indira Gandhi Have Been Elected Prime Minister?" and, mulling over my strategy in the weeks before the event, I hit upon a brilliant idea. My performance would not be marred by so much as the rustle of a turned page: I would memorize the entire three-thousand-word speech. Oh I'd bring it up to the podium with me, the same as my classmates, but while they would be forced to look down and consult their papers, I would be free to emote, to persuade, to convince the whole school that nobody was smarter or more eloquent than me. I'd show *them*, I thought, holed up night after night in my bedroom, obsessively reviewing each page, paragraph, sentence, word. I stood in front of the mirror and practiced by the hour. Maybe I'd even go into acting, I mused, resetting the stopwatch I'd swiped from my father's handkerchief drawer.

The night of the contest, I donned my best dress—a peagreen dirndl with bell sleeves—and, rigid with anticipation, sat in the backseat as Dad, Mom, and I drove down Atlantic Avenue to school. In the auditorium, kids chased one another around flicking light switches on and off, parents jostled for metal folding chairs, and PTA mothers dispensed congo bars and fruit punch from the kitchen. I made my way to the stage, greeting my classmates with the fake congeniality with which I'd already learned to mask all true feeling—"Hey, Kath!" "How's it goin', Jimbo?"—and found a seat in the semicircle of chairs fanned out across the apron. A podium loomed to the front. On a table to the side, three gold trophies—one large, one medium-sized, one small—were arranged in descending order of size. Behind them, bathed in shadow, lay a stack of Modern Library books: consolation prizes for the pathetic also-rans who didn't even place.

The background din subsided to isolated voices, then whispers, the scrape of a shoe, a cough, and finally, expectant silence. I scanned the crowd for my parents. They were in the middle of a row near the back, Mom worn out from another day of scrubbing diapers, Dad no doubt calculating the cost of a babysitter for the night. How happy, how relieved they'd be to find that their famous daughter would save them from the poorhouse! Just then, Mr. Elliot, the English teacher-moderator, tucked in the chest hairs that stuck out above the top of his tie, stepped to the front of the stage, and in his best radio announcer voice said, "Welcome, ladies and gentlemen, to the 1966 North Hampton Elementary School Oratorical Contest!"

John Demerast and Lynne Blackburn preceded me, but I was too busy imagining the deafening applause that would erupt as I accepted the largest of the gold trophies to pay much attention. When my name was called, I strode across the stage, laid my superfluous sheaf of blue-lined white paper on the podium, and confidently began. I knew exactly which words to emphasize, where to let my voice rise and fall, when to pause. My eyes swept the hall like a searchlight, carefully making contact with people on both sides of the room. The audience was in the palm of my hand. That was the beauty of it, not to be distracted for a single second by the bothersome written words.

Any fool could have predicted what happened next. Halfway through, my mind went blank: frontal-lobotomized, black-hole blank. It was like one of those moments in the privacy of my bedroom when I forgot who and where I was, except that instead it was a people-packed auditorium and about two hundred pairs of judging eyes were riveted on me. I stood paralyzed for what seemed like aeons: rivulets of icy sweat running down my side, the seconds on the giant wall clock ringing out like pistol shots, so appalled at the egregiousness of my lapse I half expected the crowd to rise up and begin stoning me, like the townsfolk in Shirley Jackson's "The Lottery."

I considered looking down to find my place, but I'd reprised my delivery so many times it seemed like cheating to consult the actual written speech. Lesser souls did that, people who hadn't practiced enough, who didn't have the wherewithal to shut themselves up for hours on end: losers. By the time I'd figured out that it was infinitely more disruptive to stand like a deer caught in headlights for sixty seconds than to rustle a page, it was too late. I fumbled the papers, brought the debacle to a limping close, and returned to my seat. For the remainder of the contest, I burned so hot with humiliation it's a wonder I didn't spontaneously combust.

The three trophies went to other, more deserving classmates: Mr. Elliot presented me with Rudyard Kipling's *Kim*. I went on to graduate as valedictorian and win the coveted American Legion award—Honesty, Loyalty, Bravery—but in my mind none of it could begin to negate my freakish, unforgivable failure. I had made a mistake, and it would shadow me forever: the black mark that had ruined my perfect record. *Kim* lay, dusty and unread, on the highest shelf of the living-room bookcase: my introduction to puberty, a ghastly memento of shame.

seven

Wandering between two worlds
One dead, one powerless to be born.
— Matthew Arnold,
"Stanzas from the Grand Chartreuse"

Thus equipped, I ventured into the world beyond North Hampton: the four-town regional school known as Winnacunnet High. Winnacunnet was located in Hampton, which, with its seven thousand inhabitants compared to North Hampton's four thousand, was to my mind a virtual metropolis. The bus still stopped across the street at the church, but instead of heading east toward the beach, now we went to the end of Post Road, turned south on Route 1, cruised through downtown Hampton—the Sugar 'n' Spice bakery, the Bib 'n' Crib, Colt's News—and, just this side of the marshes that marked the boundary with Hampton Falls, turned left on Tuck Road and went up the hill.

WHS was a soulless single-story building of brick and

glass with the caf to the left, the gym straight ahead, and to the right a series of "wings" jarringly bisected by stairwells, "lounges," and the see-through library. At the orientation assembly, at which the school mascot whooped around in buckskin breeches, feathered headdress, and a full set of war paint, I learned that Winnacunnet was the name of an Indian tribe, our anthem began "We are the Warriors, the mighty mighty Warriors," and our yearbook was entitled *Sachem*—an Algonquian word meaning "chief." In those carefree, pre-politically-correct days, my objection to a bunch of white kids pretending they were a tribe of seventeenth-century Indians was that is was simply *lame*. I had no idea the real problem was that we were hateful, oppressive bigots.

With hundreds of strange new students to make a fool of myself in front of, naturally from the first day, I felt like a complete geek: our whole freshman year, Pete Parks and I went around making fun of each other's "puddles," the telltale rings of nervous sweat that darkened the armpits of our shirts. Mrs. Valley, our French teacher, was a formidable taskmaster with black-dyed hair who we respected absolutely and who found a way in every class to mention that she had graduated from Radcliffe and whose favorite phrase was "Monsieur Parks! Mademoiselle King! Après l'école!" Pete and I were constantly passing notes saying "You have puddles!" and prodding each other's thighs with pens under our desks whenever Mrs. Valley mentioned Radcliffe, for which we had to stay after school at least once a week.

For algebra we had Miss Camp, a babe with a Southern accent, cat's-eye glasses, and orange lipstick. Everyone liked

Gloria, and we were all secretly rooting for her to get a boyfriend from among the ranks of single geometry, science, and/or English teachers. American Civ was taught by Harold Fernald, who had the face of a bulldog, a neck so fat it formed sausage-like folds, and a vivid lecturing style, with such enthusiasm for his subject that spit flew from his mouth when he spoke of Mesopotamia, the Dardanelles Straits, or the Fertile Crescent. Mr. Fernald sometimes brought in as a guest lecturer his friend Mr. Montgomery, a passionate explicator of the big bang theory. Mr. Montgomery was shaped like a bowling pin, with a small egg-like head, tiny feet, and a tummy so big the waist of his pants was up around his armpits, and we often feared that, right in front of us, he might explode himself.

WHS would have been just another run-of-the-mill, middle-America school except for one thing: an anthropological curiosity known as Brookers (after Seabrook, the town where they lived). All Brookers, both girls and boys, had been smoking cigarettes and drinking beer since the age of eight, were vicious fistfighters, and had bizarre, barely intelligible, Olde English–Appalachia-extreme-down-Maine accents that linguists had determined had remained intact since the 1700s—probably because, having been inbreeding for generations, or so the rumor went, the only time Brookers ever ventured from Seabrook was to attend high school. Brooker boys wore black loafers and white socks and packs of Luckies in their rolled-up shirtsleeves. Brooker girls wore black eyeliner and white lipstick, bleached their hair by dunking it into a sinkful of straight peroxide, and tattooed the names of their boyfriends—"Killer," "Ace"—on their biceps with crudely sharpened Bic pens, like prison inmates. Brooker girls worked after school shucking clams, Brooker boys fixed cars (Brooker houses all looked like salvage yards), and they all bore our craven scapegoating with a nobility of spirit I can only marvel at today, going about their business, ignoring our obnoxiously smirking asides, and calmly beating the living shit out of anybody who finally pushed them too far.

Lockers were assigned alphabetically, and the whole time I was in high school mine was next to that of Delwyn Knowles, a pleasant, quiet boy with three-inch sideburns who belied every Brooker stereotype and who I secretly longed to make friends with and thereby gain a window onto the Brooker psyche/way of life ("Do your mothers really sit in the front yard in their bras and play poker?" "Is it true your father sleeps with your sister?").

"Hey, Del, what's up?" I said every morning. Delwyn smiled shyly back, but I could never draw him out.

There were many options for extracurricular activities at Winnacunnet—Mathletes, the Winnacarnival Planning Committee—but I became a jock. I played halfback in field hockey and second base in softball, but it was basketball I lived and breathed for. The names of my college professors, the hotel I stayed in on my honeymoon, the faces of my coworkers from five years ago all escape me, but I still remember the starting lineup from my freshman basketball team. They should have

sent *us* to Vietnam; I'm pretty sure I would have died for
those girls. There's a photo in my senior yearbook of the
team in a huddle, my brow furrowed in such concentration I
appear to be on the verge of tears. It was that important to
me, the one sacred thing in an adolescence where I would
turn out to be otherwise pretty much hell-bent on robbing
myself of the capacity for meaning and joy.

Watching, say, the L.A. Sparks these days, in their
perspiration-wicking miracle fabrics and Nike Airstreams, I
see women's basketball has changed a bit. In the quaintly by-
gone era of my youth, we wore dark blue skirted uniforms,
made of a kind of cotton that had apparently been especially
designed to trap and hold B.O., and black low-top Converse
sneakers that must have weighed five pounds apiece. Back
then, a girls' team consisted of six players: three each of for-
wards and guards—two stationary, one "roving." The stationary guards couldn't shoot, obviously; plus, you could only
dribble three times before passing, which meant that the principal part of a game consisted of a girl pivoting uncertainly
back and forth in her dowdy uniform while her teammates
yelled, "Noreen! Over here!" or "Di! I'm wide open!" Altogether, in fact, the game was so slow that a final score of over
20 was considered high (the year I got MVP my score for the
whole season was only 99). But of course it didn't seem slow
then, and I was so proud of every one of those points I knew
many of them by heart, and often replayed them in my memory as I lay in bed at night or otherwise needed cheering up.

I loved it all: the anticipation on the day of a game; the

locker room beforehand, smelling of White Shoulders and Ban; the bus rides to and from away games, where Jill and I held court from the backseat. Basketball was one arena where we could really make our partnership shine. Jill, a stationary forward, was short and sturdy, a scrapper with a nifty left-hand layup. I played roving forward: a ball stealer with quick reflexes and a halfway decent outside shot. Our coach, Miss Ball (not a made-up name), wasn't one of those short-haired, dykey types. She had an auburn pageboy, smelled of baby powder, and wore cardigan sweaters, placketed with gros-grain ribbon, in soothing, big-sister shades of heather green and periwinkle blue. Jill and I adored her—she was one of the few teachers who didn't run the other way at the sight of the two of us together—and though her hair wasn't even really red, Jill started calling her Carrot Top. We'd be at practice reviewing one of our "plays"—which consisted of, say, half a pass and a layup—and from the back of the court you'd hear, "Okay, Carrot Top." "Get out there and fight, girls," Miss Ball urged before the opening jump. "We will, Carrot Top." Naturally I egged things on by laughing like a hyena every time the words issued from Jill's mouth.

The afternoon before the final game of the season Miss Ball took me and Jill aside. "You know darn well you two are the best players on the team, and I would have liked to nominate you for next year's co-captains," she told us. "I know you're only fooling around, but the other girls . . . they have to have people they can look up to, leaders who'll set an example for them."

We looked down at the floor and shuffled our feet.

"You know we love basketball, and you're a great coach . . ." I offered.

"I'm sorry," Jill echoed.

"Okay then," Miss Ball said, putting an arm around each of us. "Dianne and Cindy will be our co-captains. Now let's all pull together and have a great game."

"Thank you," Jill said, and then, softly, "Carrot Top."

eight

For we are not contending against flesh and
blood, but against the principalities, against
the powers, against the world rulers of this
present darkness, against the spiritual hosts of
wickedness in the heavenly places.

—Ephesians 6:12

One of the reasons I loved basketball so much was that,
like reading, it made me forget. I had finally started
wearing a bra and gotten my period—oh the horror, the embarrassment, the halting, eyes-averted conversations with my
mother!—but as of my freshman year I still hadn't so much as
been kissed, and I lived in a state of constant, mortal apprehension that I was too ugly and queer to ever have a
boyfriend. The cool kids who did drugs—Kelly Cash (later
died of cirrhosis), Alex McDonough (O.D.'ed), Michael
Tapalucci (shot to death)—hung out before the morning bell
rang by the planter in the lobby. I scurried by with my blue

binder, head down, coveting their ghostly pallor, their cheap leather jackets, the hickeys on their acne-scarred necks.

My only contact with these untouchables was Jill's older sister Mercedes. Though not a druggie herself, Mercedes was friends with the druggies, and told us of their esoteric lives as she drove us to school in a VW Bug she fueled with fifty-cent increments of gas. Mercedes wore a beige trench coat and nylons and Weejuns; and smoked Tareytons, like Crabwoman; and had the kind of cool carelessness that Fitzgerald noted in *The Great Gatsby* is possessed by the very rich. In fact, though she tolerated us on occasion, Merc hung out with rich kids (a second set of untouchables): kids from Rye Beach who went to private schools—Phillips Exeter, Deerfield Academy—and whose parents traveled, leaving nicely stocked liquor cabinets.

So one afternoon Jill called and said, "Merc has got some beer. Do you want to go down to White's Lane tonight and drink some beer?" And of course I said "Sure," thinking, Oh, by all means. Beer. That sounds good.

White's Lane was an overgrown dirt road off Route 1 in Hampton, and that night, right after supper, Mercedes and Jill and I, and a couple of older guys who were friends of Merc's, drove down there with a case of Budweiser. They say normal people don't remember their first drink—it's no red-letter day in their lives—but I remember every detail about mine: the moss-covered stone wall we parked beside, the air smelling of fresh, rain-dampened earth, the spring peepers sending up their hopeful song.

One of the guys, a hood with a package of Zig-Zags behind his ear, was up front with Mercedes, and the other, a football player with a girlfriend at Dana Hall, was in the back with me and Jill. "Here, Heath," Jill said, and handed me a brown glass bottle. I'd seen my father drink from bottles like this a hundred times: the red-and-white label, the friendly shoulders sloping up to the neck, the rounded little ridges where you put your mouth. I looked at it for a minute. Jill had already drunk beer a few times, and we'd pretended in advance, so the guys wouldn't think I was queer, to pretend I had, too. I knew this was a rite of passage, and it made me a little sad and scared to think I was leaving my childhood behind, but to say so out loud would have been even queerer. And then I took a sip: on top cool and clean, like the driest ginger ale and, underneath, a whopping poisonous aftertaste that made me want to gag.

"What do you think?" Jill said.

"Great!" I squeaked, fighting down the bile. "Yup. Always liked Bud."

I choked down another sip, turning my face to the window as I grimaced. I swallowed a third time, throat burning, eyes stinging, trying so hard not to throw up it felt like the top of my head would come off. The next sip went down a teeny bit easier. I rested for a minute, took a deep breath, garnered my strength. The next sip went down easier still.

They talk about crossing an invisible line, but there was no invisible line for me: my awakening was instantaneous and it was complete. For halfway through that first bottle, suddenly, miraculously, I was transformed. Suddenly I felt pretty, competent, at ease; I felt embraced and welcome; I suddenly realized

I *loved* Mercedes—fascinating, understanding Mercedes—and I'd never told her! "Thanks for driving!" I blurted, leaning impulsively into the front seat to give her a hug.

"Lesbo," Jill snickered, taking a swig off her own bottle. "Is this stuff bitchin' or what?"

After that, it was a laugh-fest and a love-in. Convulsing with hysterics, Jill and I sang "Swinging Along the Open Road," which we'd learned in sixth grade. Mercedes told an actually very funny story about the time she got caught smoking in the home-ec test kitchen. As for the two guys, they morphed in the space of an hour from alien creatures whose judgment I dreaded and feared into companions, equals, friends who, like me, wanted nothing more than to be touched and held and kissed. As the night progressed, things dimmed and blurred. There were flashes of getting out of the car, crashing through underbrush, leaning against the stone wall; teeth, tongues, the taste of Wrigley's; the smell of Jade East, flesh straining against cloth; dizzying, lay-down-your-life-for warmth.

Later still, I insulted everyone, got sick, and blacked out; the next morning I woke up with such a pounding hangover I thought I was going to die. I lied to my mother and father—"It was awful, right in the middle of the movie I got the flu really bad"—got put on restriction for coming in late, prayed I'd never see either of the guys again. But somehow that all seemed a paltry price to pay. Somehow it wasn't the *end* of the evening my brain focused on; it was the *beginning*. That sense of connection, of being at one with the universe, was so sublime that already I was prepared to make any sacrifice, over-

look any amount of pain to recapture it. The second I was
well enough to crawl out of bed, I dragged myself to the
phone and called Jill. "When can we do it again?" I croaked.

I didn't know that, when it came to alcohol, I was bodily
and mentally different from normal people. I didn't know
that when that first drink entered my system, I was hardwired
to want a second, and a third, and on to infinity. I didn't
know that a craving had been triggered whereby I was bound
to keep drinking until I got locked up in a mental institution
or landed in jail or died.

A normal person would regard the next two decades of
my life, scratch his or her head, and say, "Why'd you do
that? Why didn't you just stop?" But already I couldn't have
stopped. I didn't know that by taking that first drink I had
surrendered my free will: the thing that distinguishes a human being from an animal.

I don't mean I turned into some raging, teenage maniac of an
alcoholic the next day, passing out in gutters and holding up
liquor stores. But what did kick in immediately was the mental
obsession, the neurological compulsion, the nagging thought
that lay, however deeply buried, beneath every other thought:
the planning and scheming for, the distracted preoccupation
with how to get ahold of the next drink. This could have been
a problem, as the drinking age was twenty-one, and I was only
thirteen, not to mention that in New Hampshire booze was
sold only at few-and-far-between state liquor stores.

Luckily, Jill and I got our first job that summer, chamber-
maiding at the Main Beach. Plaice Cove and Little Boar's

Head were family spots farther north where the sand was strewn with picnic baskets and plastic pails but, no doubt due to its proximity to Massachusetts, the Main Beach had a titillating edge of sleaze. The air smelled of fried dough and head-shop incense, hawkers sold Grateful Dead T-shirts from the alleys, and alongside the tourists—old people thronging Giovanni's for the early-bird special, Canadian women in terry-cloth shorts shopping for spun-glass wishing wells—Hell's Angels cruised the strip, Janis Joplin played the Casino, and kids from gritty Boston suburbs like Chelsea and Malden milled through the pinball arcades selling pot.

The motel where we worked consisted of ten little white cabins, right off traffic-clogged Ocean Boulevard, where the guests seemed to do nothing but have sex. Whenever the owner, a fussbudget from Worcester, was around, we'd scrub the shower grout with toothbrushes, or stand thoughtfully back from the mirrors as if to make sure we'd gotten every last speck, and as soon as she was gone we'd flop down on the nearest bed and screech, "Gross! Did you see that pubie in the sink?" or "Eeeeewww! What about those sheets? They were all *crusty*!"

Drinking as a reward for the "pain" of such everyday activities as study or work was a notion that dawned on me early on. Nobody was supposed to actually hang out at the Main Beach, but it was easy to fudge our hours, or say, "Hey, Mom, Jill and I are going up to Bunny's after for ice cream, okay?" Instead we'd hitchhike south on Route 1, just over the state line, to a place in full-bore sleazoid Salisbury (tattoo parlors, carny-run amusement park) that probably had a name but that we referred to by the neon sign in the window: "99,000 Bottles of Cold Beer." Here, we sat on the cinderblock wall at the edge of the parking lot and waited for a likely prospect to appear: young and cute, older and horny. "Hey," Jill would yell as someone promising pulled into an empty space, "ya wanna *buyyyyyyyy*?"

The trick was to get whoever agreed to buy to also drive us back to Hampton without trying to slap the make on us. We steered clear of overt pariahs—trailer-park pervs, Neanderthal backwoodsmen—but almost everybody made some kind of move anyway: the guy from Pease Air Force Base whose wife was visiting her mother, the loser with the *Playboy* bunny decal on the bumper of his 'Vette.

"Hey, ya wanna? . . ."

"Not with *you*," Jill would sneer, grabbing our six-pack. "Come on, Heath, let's go."

Safely installed on our favorite stone wall, back at White's Lane, we'd crack our first beers. Already they went down easier. Already I could drink three or four at a whack. And already I'd come to depend on that warm, comforting glow.

It was no accident that the very first time I drank, and almost every time after, there were boys involved. For me, romance, fantasy, the pain of prospective heartache delivered the same kind of addictive rush as alcohol and, from the beginning, it presaged a love life of unmitigated disaster. My first "crush" (I didn't have crushes, I had full-flight-from-reality obsessions) was on Armand Romero, a gypsy whose family was in the hot-topping business. Dark, sweating, shirtless men; the smell of tar; gay music around a painted caravan: after the house I'd grown up in, this was a scenario that appealed to me deeply. Armand was swarthy, with chiseled cheekbones, and his status as a D student only added to the allure: perhaps I could tutor him, I thought tenderly. When he handed me the pencil I'd dropped in study hall, I was sure a marriage proposal couldn't be far behind. Instead, the very next week I spotted him behind the candy-bar machine making out with Vicki Felch, a Brooker girl with giant boobs and frosted hair.

Devastated, I developed a yen for Frankie Phelan, the star of the basketball team. Every day I took note of his outfit: Was he wearing the green sweater or the blue one? Were his stilt-like legs encased in the plaid bell-bottoms or the gray corduroys? I went to his games, I called his house and hung up when he answered, I almost had a heart attack every time I passed him in the corridor. His eyes were shifty and brown, and a barely perceptible shadow hovered above his upper lip: "Is he trying to grow a *mustache*?" I shrieked to Jill over the phone. I could, of course, have simply gone up and talked to him, but such straightforward tactics, devoid of masochism, weren't my way. I had a better idea: get falling-down drunk and show up at the next school dance.

The night was a kaleidoscope of fractured images: maroon velvet curtains drawn across the stage, Mrs. Valley wearing a chaperone corsage, a stab of sick excitement and longing as I spotted Him, towering above the crowd, wearing—oh God, I could hardly stand it—a new red pullover. As the DJ played "Searching for My Baby," my sodden brain was reduced to one thought: Frankie, Frankie, Frankie. The part in Frankie's hair, the class ring on Frankie's finger, Frankie's rodent-like teeth, which I would have lain my life down for to see up close. "Searchin', searchin' for my baby, oh yes I am . . ."

Afterward—did I ask him to meet me in the parking lot? Could I have been that drunk, a sophomore in high school?— somehow Frankie and I were sitting on the asphalt, away from the cars, beneath an outdoor basketball hoop. It was warm outside, springtime, moonlight swirling. It was the moment I'd ached for and dreamed about, together under the stars with Frankie Phelan: my boyfriend. "What do you want?" he asked. "I like you," I said, slurring my words. "I like you," eyes spinning. "I like you," head lolling, bombed. That was the last thing I remember. Frankie never talked to me again.

See, I thought. Nothing ever works out for *me.*

nine

If your eye is sound, your whole body will be
filled with light; but if your eye is bad, your
whole body will be in darkness. And if the
light in you is darkness, how great will the
darkness be.

—Matthew 6:22–23

The upheaval of the late sixties—the Age of Aquarius,
Woodstock, tuning in and dropping out—shook WHS to
its very core. After a hard-fought battle, girls won the right to
wear pants to school. Another victory by the student council
resulted in the installation of a Coke machine in the cafeteria.
Billy O'Brien, the school's token political activist, challenged
the district board of education, forced them to their knees in
a showdown over the Constitution's free-speech clause, and
was allowed to keep his sideburns.

Billy was a "leader"—passionately idealistic, an eloquent
debater, and possessed of a supreme self-confidence that made

him utterly oblivious to the opinions of others. While this allowed him to chart his own course politically, what interested me far more was his swami-like state of personal detachment. He had terrible B.O., for instance, but far from being embarrassed, he seemed to revel in the fact that people were constantly going around saying, "Gross! Would you put on some deodorant?" To my delight, in fact, Billy was fixated on all gross bodily things—zits, dandruff, phlegm—which, along with his animal smell, lent our dynamic an intriguingly sexual air.

Billy and I had bonded as lab partners in freshman earth science: heating simulated lava over a Bunsen burner; dissing Herbert Holmes, our benighted teacher. But our pact was sealed the afternoon he invited me to his house in Hampton and I met his family. Billy lived in a sprawling Cape with multiple TVs, two book-strewn bathrooms, and a fully stocked larder. The first time I went over, his mother invited me to stay for dinner, his father nicknamed me Feathers, and his six younger brothers and sisters reported that on Wednesdays the cleaning woman stood in the middle of Billy's bedroom, shook her head in disgust, and uttered a single word: "Slob!" I practically moved in on the spot.

Mr. and Mrs. O'Brien were also parents, teachers, and friends, but it was as hosts that they really shone. Birthdays, graduations, the summer solstice—in the O'Brien household, no occasion was too trifling for a party. Mr. O'Brien had a unique personality, and he'd coined a language all his own. When he wanted you to get out of the way, he exclaimed, " 'K'out, 'k'out, 'k'out some more!" and, to him, people didn't laugh, they "kink-kinked." Aftershave was "smell-well," chicken "bones and feathers"; tuna—because they'd found insect parts in it—"moth meat." A math instructor, he told fractured jokes with punch lines like "Pi are not square, pie are round!" after which he'd kink-kink. He said "JelLO!" instead of Hello and distributed copies of the *JelLO Journal*, a newsletter he published on a mimeograph machine and that consisted of late-breaking stories—"Tooth Fairy Visits Tess," "Markie to Attend Camp Fatima!"—about his wife and children.

One Saturday morning I arrived to find the family knee-deep in preparations for the annual Flag Day shindig. "Helpy-selfy, eat all!" Mr. O'Brien greeted me. He was pacing the kitchen, an apron over his Chinese-red Bermuda shorts: smoking cigarettes, drinking coffee, reaching around whoever was in the way—" 'K'out, Feathers"—to answer the telephone.

"Jello? . . . Tess! It's Lindy Lou! . . . She'll be right down, Lindy. By the way, we're hosting a small gathering tonight and you're more than welcome . . ."

"Jello? . . . Eric! It's Skid!" (Skid was Mr. O'Brien's nickname for Eric's twelve-year-old friend Davy Rowe) ". . . He'll be here in a minute, Davy. Feel free to come on by later, there'll be food and very possibly some beverage . . ."

"Jello! . . . Yes, you can come by and read the meter any time, we're home all day. As a matter of fact, if it's toward late afternoon you might want to stay for a bit . . ."

During the course of the day Mr. O'Brien made a "race car" centerpiece for the picnic table—pineapple wheels, a tomato-head driver. He made endless trips uptown in the yellow Comet (which we, of course, called the Vomit) for ice, charcoal, napkins, toothpicks, potato chips, tonic, beer. Everybody else pitched in, too: vacuuming, doing laundry, supervising the younger kids; Mrs. O'Brien was in the kitchen all afternoon making macaroni salad, tossed salad, chicken wings. Toward dusk he ran uptown one last time for lighter fluid: we covered the backyard picnic tables with red-and-white-checked oilcloth, set out paper plates and plastic cups, arranged the Kon-Tiki candles. That night he presided over the grill, turning out heaping platters of cheeseburgers and hot dogs while we milled around smoking, chatting, nibbling.

At nine-thirty, he was emptying ashtrays, tossing paper plates into the trash, scraping the grill. "Thanks so much for having me!" I said, preparing—finally—to take my leave. Surely I'd worn out my welcome this time, I was thinking, surely I'd eaten too much, surely I'd stayed too long.

"Come by tomorrow!" Mr. O'Brien said. "Markie's graduating from kindergarten. We're hosting a little party . . ."

Mrs. O'Brien, too, was relaxed, gracious, and welcoming to a degree that would have been remarkable in anybody, never mind a woman who had gone back to school to get her teaching credential, worked full-time, and had seven children and innumerable of their friends to keep track of, cook for, and clean up after. Encouraging without being intrusive, motherly but never overbearing, she was a foil for Mr. O'Brien; a center of calm in a house where everyone seemed supported, but everyone seemed free to breathe. The O'Briens accepted me, they acknowledged me, they widened the circle and let me in. They became a kind of second, surrogate family, the lodestar by which I have measured hospitality ever since—and always found it slightly wanting.

I had an on-again, off-again crush on Billy all through high school. But in the end, I became even better friends with his two-years-younger-than-us twin brothers, Terrence and Thomas. Billy, sensitive though he could be, was geared toward the outside world, but Terry and Tommy were introverts like me. Upstairs, we had barbecues and birthday parties; downstairs, we holed up in what Mrs. O'Brien drily referred to as the Den of Iniquity: a low-ceilinged cellar furnished with a sprung-seated sofa, overstuffed armchairs, and a cast-off coffee table littered with rolling papers, burned-down cones of sandalwood incense, and candles stuck in empty Molson Golden bottles. In summer we fanned our faces with dog-eared copies of *On the Road* and *Tropic of Cancer*; in winter we huddled around the woodstove; and, along with assorted girlfriends, boyfriends, and stray hangers-on, it seems as if we spent the better part of our youth down there: talking about books, hatching plans, and listening to *Highway 61 Revisited* and *Blonde on Blonde* and *Blue*.

Thomas was smart (the type that teachers wring their hands over, sighing about lost potential), with the kind of stubborn intensity, tortured charisma, and disdain for authority that make a person almost wholly unfit for life in the real world. He had extraordinarily deep, almost transparent blue eyes, and in the middle of a conversation, you'd look over and he'd be sitting there just sort of staring at a corner of the ceiling, except you could tell that he was gazing at some point way beyond the ceiling, that he'd checked out to some other, better realm, out there in the ether. "Earth to Tom," Terry would say, and Tommy would come to with a little smirk and say, "How's it goin', Heath?" or "Who wants to smoke some weed?"

Guilt-ridden, conflicted, God-haunted, Tommy was the first in a long line of Irish Catholic boys I'd have a thing for. Cocky but sensitive, cynical but capable of startling bursts of tenderness, Tom was the kind of muscular, rugged "guy" who could fix cars and frame houses, but who'd also make you a birthday card out of a napkin—a cut-out photo and a poem written in blue crayon—or a bookcase with a little door in the middle of the bottom shelf that when you opened it was painted in red, "To Heather on her seventeenth birthday, with all my love . . ."

Plus—my major prerequisite in a friend—he had the black, self-deprecating sense of humor that comes from living in almost unalloyed pain. In between making fun of ourselves, each other, and everyone we knew, we spent hours talking on the phone and writing long rambling letters to each other: complaining, commiserating, trying to figure things out.

Terry was everything you'd want in a best friend: schemer, snooper, dead-on mimic, ace driver, and possessed of an Eddie Haskell streak that made parents love him (parents tended—rightfully—to mistrust Thomas). Terry suffered from his share of dark moods, but he also had the kind of emotional resourcefulness and very slight Gladys Kravitz streak that, luckily for me, made him a natural caretaker.

One afternoon when we were down in the Den of Iniquity, and I was suffering from yet another broken heart, Terry opened one of his trillions of books of poetry. "Here, honey, this will cheer you up," he said and, in his most sonorous, solicitous voice, began reading, "I have eaten/the plums/that were in/the icebox . . ."

"That's beautiful, Terrence," I sniffed. "Go on."

"William Carlos Williams," he replied, taking a hit off his cigarette. "So did you let him touch your boobs?"

Terry was also, though he didn't officially come out for several more years, very clearly gay: even at thirteen, he was interested in things no straight boy would have been—picking flowers, setting a nice table. Nanny, Mrs. O'Brien's mother and another indispensable member of the clan, doted on him: "Doesn't he have the devil in his eye?" she'd cluck (little did she know). Nanny worked at the Sugar 'n' Spice bakery and lived in an uptown apartment that was decorated with wax-fruit baskets, plastic crucifixes, and photos of her seemingly innumerable grandchildren. Terry would go up there Saturday afternoons and help her bake—blond brownies, sugar-sprinkled apple pie—partly because he liked to bake and partly because Nanny provided endless material for the impersonations and monologues he was always honing. "What do they call those now, Terry, *bell*-bottoms?" he'd say, cocking an eyebrow and putting a finger to an imaginary Nanny dimple. "Hmmmmmm. *Dif*ferent . . ."

Terrence was one of those people who is naturally good, naturally thoughtful, naturally happy, and he was always especially kind and gentle to me. And while in many ways Tom and Terry were totally different, they were also totally devoted to each other. I would go on to have a long, long history with both of them, and though they are no longer part of my daily life, even now I keep them always in my heart.

Due to its stunning shoreline and relative proximity to Boston, these days the area where I grew up is prime real estate in which a rundown ranch house can fetch upwards of a third of a million dollars. By the time I was a junior in high school, however, I wanted nothing more than to escape. I'd been born in the wrong street, the wrong town, the wrong *state* even—why did I have to come from boring *Cow* Hampshire instead of some exciting, twentieth-century place like New York or California?

Partly this was garden-variety adolescent discontent, and partly it was alcohol already doing its nefarious work. When Hitchcock's *Shadow of a Doubt* came to the Ioka in Exeter, and Terry and I went to see it, my favorite scene was the one where Uncle Charlie (played by Joseph Cotten) has a heart-to-heart with his young niece in the 'Til Two lounge. "Do you know the world is a foul sty?" he asks her. "Do you know if you ripped the fronts off houses, you'd find swine?" Already I so thoroughly identified with that line of thinking it took me a minute to realize it was meant to show that Uncle Charlie (later exposed as a serial murderer of helpless widows) was *deranged*.

Somewhere around this time, I lost my virginity (giant letdown), started smoking, and developed an entirely bogus "political" conscience that was not in the least about anybody else but was instead all about me. I read Jack London and John Steinbeck, and suddenly the union meetings my father attended, about which I had never displayed the slightest curiosity, acquired a veneer of gritty glamour. How well *we* knew the crack of the foreman's whip, I thought bitterly, lounging in my bedroom and lighting another clandestine cigarette. I went door-to-door canvassing for Eugene McCarthy with Billy, but all I really cared about was whether we were going to make out at the end of the night. I claimed to be afire with the sixties ideals of peace and love, but what I really liked about the sixties was that they were lulling me into thinking that my already over-the-top drinking was normal. (A couple of years later I participated in a takeover of the Seabrook Nuclear Power Plant, and was appalled at getting arrested and locked up in the local armory for three days—not because I'd have a criminal record, or would lose my job, or the New Hampshire seacoast might be destroyed if there was a nuclear accident, but because there wasn't any booze in there. It was a dismal time, with groups of people off in a corner performing tai chi, or forlornly singing "We Shall Overcome," or giving lessons in massage.)

With what I liked to consider my vast range of reading, I fancied myself a bit of a philosopher, though in reality my "philosophy"—basically that I was confused and lonely—consisted of little more than a handful of random quotes. Inspired by Charles Manson's Helter Skelter rampage, I filched a can of black enamel from my father's workbench one Saturday afternoon, snuck upstairs, and, drips cascading, proceeded to deface the pink walls of my bedroom with some favorite sayings.

"Heather!" my mother said when she came in the next day with a basket of freshly folded laundry and saw what I'd done.

"Don't worry, I'll be gone in a few years," I waved her off, gazing about in satisfaction at the thoughts that would keep me company till then: Rousseau's "Man is born free, but is everywhere in chains" (I had that one right; in my case, I was forging them myself); Sartre's "Hell is other people" (I should have tried looking in the mirror); and, over the closet where I could see it from my bed, a little bon mot I'd composed myself: "Dreams suck."

Fifteen years old, and dreams sucked. Billy's activism was based on youthful ideals but, for someone that age, I had already lost an awful lot of hope.

ten

———

A perverse and crooked generation seeks after
a sign, and no sign shall be given to it
except the sign of the prophet Jonah.

—Matthew 16:4

At a bar with college friends, my mother had ordered a
glass of milk (how she ever ended up with me for a child,
I'll never know), and though my father certainly enjoyed a few
beers, he never displayed the telltale signs of an alcoholic. So it
was hard to know from their generally stoic silence what my
parents thought of my all-too-obvious drinking. Never much
good at covering up, I exhibited red-flag going-down-the-tubes
behavior—staggering home, leaving empties on the front lawn,
passing out at the dinner table—with complete abandon and
very few disciplinary repercussions.

One night Jill's sister Rita ended up spending the night
and somehow threw up out my bedroom window. The next

morning I came downstairs to find my father hosing off the dining-room window below.

"Oh my God," I said, "did . . . ?"

"The philodendron needed watering anyway," he noted dryly. "Boy you and your friends sure seem to get a lot of flu."

Did they not notice? I wondered. Or were they just embarrassed—or scared—for me? I should have been scared for myself: with family ties, moral code, and self-preservation instinct eroding by the minute, I discovered LSD. When a friend of Terry's and mine got pregnant and moved out of her parents' house, we quickly made her apartment our weekend headquarters. We'd show up Friday nights with a gallon of contraband Gallo—"I'm gonna help Stephanie with the baby again, okay Mom?"—start rolling joints, and drop a couple of tabs of windowpane. In spite of her own burgeoning drug habit, Stephanie was quite responsible, with a well-kept house, stacks of color-coded baby clothes, and an abundant supply of snacks. There we'd sit, the kid (thankfully) sleeping in the other room, as we reported on our hallucinations—"Oh wow, man, look, the wall's *meeellltttting*"—or moronically contemplating, say, a Triscuit: "It's so . . ." somebody would say, and after half an hour somebody else would say, ". . . *wheat*."

One night Terr and I left Stephanie's around two, went down to the beach, and walked up and down the boardwalk till dawn. Mesmerized by the pebbly texture, the whole time I trailed my hand along the concrete retaining wall—back and forth, back and forth—and when the sun came up, the tips of my fingers were all covered in blood.

It was the first time I'd ever stayed out all night without letting my mother know where I was. "Thank God!" she said, her voice uncharacteristically shaky, when I called her from the Sea Tern Donuts phone booth. In school, we'd been reading *Walden*, and as I waited for her to pick me up, I could only pity her small, provincial existence, so sadly devoid of the horizon-broadening experiences I myself was enjoying. "Mom?" I asked as I got in the car and noticed her hands—no doubt from a sleepless night of worry—tense on the wheel. "Do you lead a life of . . . quiet desperation?"

I'm sure there are all kinds of interesting psychological explanations of why I never had children, but they all probably boil down to this: terror that I'd get one exactly like me.

One highlight of my teenage years was the birth of my sister Meredith, whom I, in a fit of Louisa May Alcott–induced sappiness, nicknamed Little Meddy. Knowing the hellish future that awaited her as the baby of what by this time I'd in my charitable way begun to think of as the world's most fucked-up family, I liked to hold Little Meddy in my arms, feeling motherly and protective; cuddle up with her on the rug in front of the fireplace (the house's one guaranteed warm spot); or lie down on the couch and squeeze her in beside me like a heating pad.

Meddy's size, in fact, was to my mind her best attribute, and as soon as she was old enough to walk and understand simple commands, I trained her as my personal assistant. "I don't mind babysitting at all," I'd assure my mother, then lie on the couch like a pasha watching *Mr. Ed* and *Green Acres* while Little Meddy fetched me pillows, blankets, and grilled cheeses cut on the diagonal.

"Crispy on the outside, but don't burn it," I'd call languidly as she toddled, her head barely up to the top of the stove, in the kitchen. "Is that enough butter?" she'd lisp, handing me a neatly folded napkin and a plate with a perfectly done sandwich and a sliced-up dill pickle on it. "Very good, Jeeves," I'd say, patting her downy head. "You may bring me a dish of chocolate ice cream when I'm done."

Winnacunnet High's class-of-'70 graduation was scheduled to take place on a Saturday afternoon, outside on the football field, and in honor of the "new beginnings" and "thresholds of a new life" and "journeys of a thousand miles that begin with the first step" that I'd been hearing about for weeks, I drank a pint of Southern Comfort, smoked a couple of joints, and dropped half a tab of acid beforehand. Terry left me off in the parking lot behind school. "I'll meet you out here after, Heath," he said as I half fell out of the Vomit. "Heath? Oh shit, I knew I shouldn't have made that last one so strong . . ."

In the auditorium Mr. Hawley, the principal, was lining up pairs of students in alphabetical order as I stumbled around putting my gown on backward and draping the tassel from my mortarboard across my upper lip like a mustache. My marching partner was Delwyn Knowles—the mild-mannered Brooker whose locker had been next to mine—and the thought that, after four years of such intimacy, we might never meet again made me suddenly sentimental. "Del!" I bawled, grabbing his hairily tattooed arm as we filed out,

"I've alwayshh liked you. Isn't it shaaaaad we never got to be friends? . . ."

Outside in the stands—the audience a molten, shifting sea—I lost all track of time. There were speeches, with people laughing at things that weren't funny. There were long, bor- ing songs by the school band. There was movement: the swish of gowns, the back of Patricia Kenney's head. After a while the fresh air sobered me up enough to realize the sky was looking sort of . . . dark. As a matter of fact, it dawned on me, thunder was cracking, lightning was flashing, and it was pouring rain. Apparently I'd already gone up to get my diploma, because the fake leather was running, making blue rivulets across the words "Heather Donnellan King, with Highest Honors . . ."

For a second, I almost felt like crying. Then I raised my face to the sky, ecstatically licking the cold drops splashing off my cheeks and chin. "Is this fuckin' great or what?" I slurred, poking Delwyn in the ribs. "A thunderstorm for graduation. I wonder if it's some kind of, like . . . sign?"

eleven

The voice of my beloved!
Behold he comes,
leaping upon the mountains,
bounding over the hills.

—Song of Solomon 2:8

So far I'd slept with three people. David Hinchey, the first, had been "normal," a Bowdoin student who was kind to his mother, picked me up in his car—on time—and took me out on dates. It had all been very linear and by the book: date, kiss, pet, go to bed. I'd wanted a boyfriend so badly I was surprised how dull I'd found it to actually have one. Not just the sex, but Dave as a whole: I couldn't really relate to someone who wasn't tortured and miserable. Then there'd been Rudy de Roy, a rich kid from Rye Beach who played rugby and went to private school. Sex with Rudy had at least been a little livelier, but he hadn't been tormented enough to truly connect with, either. The third person I'd slept with had been Sawyer Clark, whom I'd known since second grade. Sawyer I was not even marginally attracted to—he was hairless and somewhat effeminate—but I liked him "as a person" and somehow we got into a routine where I'd go over to his house after school and we'd have this purely recreational sex. Looking back, it was such a bizarre arrangement I almost can't believe it, but two or three times a week we'd get together and have completely passionless, robotic sex. No emotional attachment, no sense that sex is a kind of sacred mutual trust, no thought for the fact that I could have gotten pregnant. It was like we were practicing for when each of us found someone we really liked.

It had to happen. I had to fall in love. It happened that very summer.

The day after graduation, five other girls and I rented a house down at the beach. It was a shingled A-frame between Rocky Bend and the old coast guard station, not far from where the surfers hung out. In spite of the fact that the water was frigidly cold at all times, New Hampshire had a small but dedicated cadre of these hardy souls, very cliquey with their vans and wet suits and distracted gazes as they scanned the horizon for swells. There was Randy Radkay, who owned the surf shop at the foot of Winnacunnet Road and gave a report—"The waves are *up*!"—every morning on the local radio station. There were the three blond Zetterburg brothers, good-looking enough to be movie stars. There was J. D. Forsberg, a big rangy wiseass who'd played football in high school and whose father was a building contractor around town.

I usually gave cliques of any kind a wide berth (I never stopped to think that in a way I belonged to one myself), but one surfer I knew and liked was Steve Nelson. Steve had hair like an African-American's, except it was dark blond, and he was usually twirling a corkscrew of it around his finger and insulting someone. An only child with a love-hate relationship with his mother—an older woman whom everyone else found perfectly pleasant and unobjectionable but whom Steve referred to as Psycho—he was a blast to hang out with: we'd once dropped some acid and spent hours riffing on the contents of the O'Briens' refrigerator: improvising little skits about clam dip and Cheez Whiz and rolling on the floor laughing. At any rate, I'd been living at the beach only a couple of weeks when, riding my bike to the store for cigarettes one afternoon, I ran into him down by the seawall.

"Quuglyarded!" he yelled when he spotted me ("Quuglyarded"—a combination of "queer," "ugly," and "retarded"—was our term of endearment for each other).

I wheeled over. Beside Steve stood a tallish guy with blue-green eyes, long, lean muscles, and shoulder-length, blond-streaked hair. He was wearing a wet suit but he didn't have that obnoxious, holier-than-thou surfer look on his face. He had a cute little sunburned nose. He looked friendly and boyish and slightly goofy, his board tucked under his arm like a mutant flipper.

I did what I always did when I wanted to impress a guy, which was to completely ignore *him*, then demonstrate my desirability by being as sarcastic as possible to whoever *else* happened to be present. "Hey, Steve," I snorted, "what're ya . . . *hangin' ten*? Maybe havin' an . . . *endless summer*? Is everything . . . *tubular*?"

"Fuck you," Steve said. "Allen, meet my friend Heather."

"We're going for pizza if you want to come," Allen said. "Come"—and for the next four years I was gone.

I don't know whether it was just the timeless, universally happy fact that young people travel in packs, or the peculiar conventions of the sixties, but I can't remember our union being impeded by any of the tortuously labyrinthine conventions of modern-day "dating." We hung out: in the back of someone's van, in the basement of somebody's parents' house, on the beach. We were with other people, we were alone, we talked. Allen had a sense of his own worth, the ability to go his own way, and, like everybody I've ever been drawn to, a unique way of expressing himself: "Such is life and life is such." "Happy Hampton Beach" was "most decent"; the waves on a given day "most righteous." "Times been busy and they's been fun," he wrote on a postcard from Montauk, return address "Larry McSweeney, Lower Norwichville, Outer Mongolia." He had a car, a white '65 Falcon he called the Falcoon. He dressed in a very cool, understated way. He listened to all this great music: Traffic, the James Gang, Cream.

Who knows how it happens? Who can remember the exact moment when you tie yourself to the stake and hand the other person a match? All I know is that the sight, smell, or touch of Allen made me feel as if I were being simultaneously jolted with electricity and injected with morphine—and, miraculously, he seemed to feel that way about me, too. Quivering, sweating, melting for each other, we drove around the beach in the Falcoon, pulling over every five minutes to kiss. We pooled our money, hitchhiked to Ken's Deli in Boston, and split a piece of $1.75 cheesecake, feeding forkfuls to each other over a corner table. In the back pocket of my jeans, I carried a bottle of Silk of Intimate, a perfume that looked like melted pearls, with which, watching from the seawall as he surfed, I drenched my wrists and neck.

Allen seemed to understand my apprehension of some other plane than the one we lived in, a parallel universe reigned by peace and harmony. We talked about this haltingly, though we had neither a name for it nor a language in which to discuss it. We sensed there was something between us—sacred, huge—that was part of this transcendent whole. One afternoon when we'd been together a couple of months and were walking along the beach, he put a name to it: love. We were in *love*! Spoken aloud, the word was blinding, explosive. We trembled in its presence, walked around in circles shaking our heads and laughing. We were shell-shocked, dazed at our good fortune.

In a friend's workshop, Allen built us a bed frame of rough pine planks. Lying in it, I memorized him, traced his contours as if they formed a map to my own psyche, studied his face as if it held the secrets of the universe, gazed into his eyes as if I were peering through a microscope. If they lined up a million sets of hands, I'd know which ones were yours, I told him. It's since come to my attention that many people have an odd approach to sex: they couple, enjoy a brief period of communal rest, then get up and, say, do the laundry.

My idea was very different. My idea was to bolt the door, close the shades, and come up for air maybe a couple of months later—and even then only for enough groceries and booze to last a couple months more. It wasn't just the sex, it was the "romance" (or my idea of romance at the time): the desire to disappear, to check out, to merge with someone else. At Allen's rented beach cottage, with its sandy linoleum floors and flimsy towels, we cooked hot plate Rice-A-Roni and listened to *Gasoline Alley* and made love so often, and at such length, it's a wonder we didn't get bedsores.

It was obsessive and self-annihilating and way too intense to last, but it was also the real thing. I know because we kept taking each other's hands and gazing into each other's eyes and he'd say, "I don't know, I feel as if I love . . . everyone." And I'd say, "I know. It's like our love radiates out to . . . the whole world." No matter what happens afterward, that's the real thing.

I couldn't have asked for more, and yet somehow, true to form, even before the summer was out I was managing to find some very small flies in the ointment. I thought *I* was self-absorbed, for example, but surfers, it soon transpired, were in a class by themselves, prattling on endlessly about swells, breaks, some mysterious place they called "outside." When the waves were up, they dropped everything, grabbed their boards, and headed to the beach like lemmings. Craving undivided attention at all times, I found such behavior in a boyfriend extremely distressing. Also, though I tried my best, I could never quite make it as surfer chick. I pretended to be interested in the best way to wax a board, I wore a choker of puka shells, I slathered myself with oil from a brown plastic bottle of Hawaiian Tropic, but the whole time I would really rather have been reading.

I couldn't see that if I'd loved Allen the way I professed to, I would have been glad he had something that made him so happy. I couldn't see that I was jealous of his surfing because I didn't have anything of my own. I couldn't see I wanted him to fill a void that no human being can fill for another. I couldn't see any of that, because I was in love, love, love. And everyone knows that love is blind—maybe not so much about the other person as ourselves.

twelve

Show me thy ways, O Lord,
teach me thy paths.
Lead me in thy truth, and teach me.

—Psalm 25

With my National Honor Society standing, I probably could have gotten into an Ivy League school, but God forbid I should have set my sights too high: that fall I started my first semester at the University of New Hampshire. State college notwithstanding, it was a lovely campus: graceful brick buildings, wide green lawns, a dairy barn that sold homemade ice cream in old-fashioned flavors like peppermint stick and frozen pudding. Not that any of that made much of an impression on me: my main thought was, Now that I'm on my own, I can get blitzed whenever I want.

First-year students were required to stay in a dorm. Mine was called Huddleston, and my roommate was Karin White, a friend from high school. Karin was a good-natured gal with wealthy parents; an art student who signed her name with a happy face beside it and suffered my black moods and sarcastic asides with the kind of good-natured grace I was utterly unable to muster myself. Dorm life called for a level of "joining up," an abandonment to the female herd from which I instinctively recoiled. I have always had great, bosom girlfriends, and I have always found large *groups* of girls extremely creepy. Maybe I was dealt less than my share of estrogen, or maybe growing up with so many brothers ruined me for the girly world, but all that squealing and chirping and exchanging of beauty tips only made me want to head for the nearest construction site and shoot the breeze with some wisecracking, down-to-earth guys.

In particular of course I wanted to head for Allen, and "going to college" was a term I immediately began to use quite loosely. My first semester I went to classes, paying the scantest of attention and getting my usual more or less straight A's, and divided the rest of my time between Allen's apartment at the beach, the spots on the beach where Allen surfed, the construction sites where Allen worked as a carpenter, and Dracut, Massachusetts, home of Allen's family: his chain-smoking mom, Bev; Jim, his used-car-salesman dad; and his five brothers and sisters. (Allen not only came from Massachusetts, he'd been raised Catholic, two more points I considered decidedly in his favor.)

When apart we wrote letters. Palpitating in front of my post-office box, I tore his open: "Because I have no news of great importance (or little for that matter) this message of joy will be brief but meaningful: I love you." After a visit to the dentist: "The killer man got me. I don't even know what he did, I think he pulled one, but whatever it fucking killed me, so I know I will die, farewell my one true love . . ." On Valentine's Day, a homemade heart: "Sorry about the green ink but I didn't have any red, I cut this out all by myself from my chest just exclusively for you . . ."

Toward March, we were hanging out one weekend in my dorm room when he said, "Hey, Betty" (we were calling each other Betty and Buster Brown at the time), "I'm gonna go surfing in Puerto Rico for a month. Ya wanna come?" I didn't need any urging. Tropical island, balmy trade winds, conch dinners under the stars: I could see it all. It felt very hip to be packing my bags, getting a ride down to Logan, flying together.

When we arrived, however, Rincón turned out to be my worst nightmare come true, a mecca for wave worshippers, crawling with surfers from both coasts with their golden tans, their zinc-covered noses, their girlfriends who spent their time stringing African beads or weaving hammocks out of hemp. We rented a pink stucco house with a dirt trail leading down to the ocean. We woke to the sound of crowing cocks. We ate hard white rolls and hunks of orange cheese and sardines with juice from the lemons we picked from the tree in our backyard squeezed over them. But most of the time we, or at least I, drank: Red Stripe beer, Cuba libres. At dusk, everybody gathered on the patio of the local store—supposedly to watch the sun set, though I was way more interested in downing the shot-sized paper soufflé cups of 151 rum you could buy over the counter for a quarter apiece.

When I'd first started drinking, alcohol had calmed my fears, but now it was starting to make me paranoid. Allen was in heaven, running off every morning with his cronies, but I focused instead on the cockroaches in the bathtub, the lecherous locals, the hours of unstructured time. As I lay on the sand with my book—hungover, alone—the sun beat down like a bludgeon and the waves foamed in, hissing like snakes. There was something sinister in the air: no sky should have been that blue, it seemed to me; no water that warm. There'd be a price to pay for such bounty, I kept thinking. There'd be a terrible, terrible price.

One day, snorkeling for shells, I looked through my mask to find the ocean floor covered with spiny sea urchins. It didn't occur to me that I was only in chest-deep, that I could tread water, that I could easily sidestroke (the one stroke I'd mastered at Camp Gundalow) in to shore. All I knew was that there was nowhere to stand and nobody to call for help. Hyperventilating with panic, snorkel forgotten, for a minute I literally thought I might die. I eventually spotted a tiny space of free sand—big enough to accommodate one foot—and paddled my way to safety.

But those few seconds of panic were grooved into my brain. Beneath the surface alcoholic haze, that was the way I felt all the time. There was no safe harbor, no sanctuary, no solid ground. For the rest of the trip, I chalked it up to being away from home. But the truth was I felt that way all the time.

* * *

Back at college, I showed off my early-season tan, resumed my studies, and ended my first year having made the dean's list both semesters. Ensconcing myself at Allen's beach cottage for the summer, one concern loomed large: money. I was running low, and with the flair for living up to my potential that would soon become a trademark, I got a job: waitressing at the Seagull Diner.

The Seagull was in Kittery, Maine, just across the bridge from Portsmouth, New Hampshire: having never gotten it together to learn how to drive, I hitchhiked the fifteen miles every day for my three-to-eleven shift. Inside, the place was all stainless steel and rounded glass-block corners, with a row of stools upholstered in maroon leather, a sea-green Waring blender to mix frappés in, and a menu featuring Westerns and BLTs and French toast with sausage that could be ordered at any hour of the day or night. The Seagull was owned by Jimmy Canty—an aging hipster in black-rimmed glasses who spent most of his time at Fisherman's Pier, his other, more lucrative restaurant in Portsmouth—but it was presided over by Ma, a big-boned, big-hearted old gal with a hunchback who'd spent so much time on her perch behind the register it looked like she'd been born there and would very likely also breathe her last while doling out toothpicks and ringing up one final guest check from that battered old captain's chair.

From the beginning, I was way too ADD to be a decent waitress. I'd start getting rolls for the people in the first booth, then decide to grab salad for the people in the second and forget the rolls till the first party was halfway through their meal; squeeze in a trip to the microwave to nuke a bowl of soup for one table while I should have been getting dessert for another; stop halfway to the kitchen for a couple of tapioca puddings, thinking it would save time in the long run, and let someone else's turkey club get cold.

I was terrified (with good reason) of not doing a good enough job, creeping about at all times in cringing fear of getting yelled at or fired by the harmless Ma, but at the same time I had no grasp whatever of the concept of "service" and considered it a gross insult that the people I waited on thought I cared what, when, and whether they ate. I scowled at the locals in John Deere caps who lined the counter and considered it a hilarious joke to call me "Smiley" as they called for a coffee refill. I rolled my eyes at the slutty biker girls who wanted extra ice for their Cokes, the lard-ass mothers who requested salad dressing on the side, the cheapskate church group that wanted separate checks. "What do you recommend?" a tourist who was taking way too much time perusing the pie case once asked. "How about *leaving?*" I snapped. It was the worst possible combination: not being any good at the work and yet considering it beneath me. I was already putting alcohol (not to mention romance) before school, career, and future, already beginning to be stuck, and nothing illustrated it better than the fact that I would support myself by waitressing for the next fifteen years.

The only thing that made it bearable was that when my shift was over, I'd walk outside to the parking lot and Allen would be waiting in the Falcoon. "Hi, Peantie," he'd say—he'd taken to calling me Peantie, a variation of Peanut I'm embarrassed to admit—and I'd look into those dreamy blue eyes and taste the salt on his neck and melt into his arms. "Did you bring any . . . ?" I'd remember to ask then, praying he'd stopped at Richardson's before crossing the bridge.

And, as he reached into the backseat and handed me an ice-cold Heineken or Löwenbräu or Bass Ale, I'd remember that, in spite of everything, I truly was the luckiest girl in the world.

thirteen

And I said, O that I had wings like a dove.
For then I would fly away and be at rest.
Lo, then I would wander far off,
and remain in the wilderness.

         —Psalm 55

At the beginning of my sophomore year I moved to New-market, a mill town south of Durham. It wasn't the launching of the Apollo 16, the arrest of Andreas Baader, or the Watergate break-in that made the biggest impression on me that year. It was the lowering of the drinking age from twenty-one to eighteen by the New Hampshire state legislature, an event that permitted me to immediately adopt the local hippie bar as my home away from home, a place called The Cave. The Cave was a cozy spot with creaky wood floors, spider plants in macramé holders, and an unbelievably slutty barmaid named Donna. Here, I proceeded to while away hundreds of hours that could have been more profitably dedicated to my education draining pitchers of beer, loudly ridiculing the other patrons, and thoroughly neglecting my homework. Rob—the owner and a dilettante biker himself—tended bar in the afternoons and could sometimes be coaxed into a game of Scrabble. "Miss me?" I'd ask, sliding onto my barstool. "Not really," he'd roll his eyes. "Aren't you supposed to be going to school?" The Cave was handily located directly across the street from my apartment, and on the rare occasions when I wasn't actually in the bar myself, I sat with a pair of binoculars by the front window, keeping watch to see who went in and out.

With varying degrees of consistency and longevity, Terry, Tom, Pete Parks, and Jill also attended UNH. Someone was always dropping by the apartment or into The Cave, making for one big communal never-ending party. I liked living in Newmarket. The crabby, cigar-smoking cook at Jake's Luncheonette served up the perfect hangover meal: a grilled-cheese sandwich and an ice-cold raspberry-lime rickey. The old Italian lady at Marelli's Fruit and Real Estate sold newspapers, cigarettes, and fifty-three-cent GIQs (Giant Imperial Quarts) of Black Label. The Cave served only beer and wine, but for hard liquor, there were the American Legion, the Elks, and the Polish Club, all of which, at Tommy's behest, we eventually joined and became members of good standing. It was at the Polish Club that we met Johnnie Hayes, a foreman at a local shoe factory. Johnnie was devoted to his cat, Max, recited Shakespeare soliloquies when in his cups—"The sound and the fury, signifying nothing" was a favorite at last call—and

drove us around to bluegrass festivals in his maroon Econo-
line van. We all became great fans of Bill Monroe and Peter
Rowan and thought nothing of setting off en masse for the
Berkshires or upstate New York or Castleton, Vermont, to
pay homage.

Terry had come out by this time and taken up with a
wounded-dove, Lord Byron type named Jeff (who was such a
hopeless alcoholic that when we heard a few years later he'd
died, we didn't even bother asking why), and I'd started
cooking. For a time in the early seventies, *The Vegetarian Epi-
cure* was my bible, and I was always whipping up batches of
soupe à trois champignons and *crème de la Irena*, and hosting dinner
parties for Allen and Terry and Jeff and Hayes and Jill and
Tommy and whoever Tommy's girlfriend was at the time.

In a way these were the "best" years of my drinking. I
would always hang out in bars; always be looking for a surrogate family to give me the warmth I craved, and this was as
close as I ever came to getting it. Even so, underneath I was
dissatisfied, itchy, restless. Surely somewhere, in some faraway Other Place—Chapel Hill, North Carolina; San Fran-
cisco; India—things would be better, people would be nicer,
the world wouldn't so constantly let me down.

Perhaps that dissatisfaction explains why there was one
more sign-of-the-times activity at which I became adept during my college years: hitchhiking. I'd hitchhiked locally since
high school, but I'm talking now about looking for America,
solidarity with the masses, weeks-long sojourns that required
backpacks and mess kits and Frostline sleeping bags. Terrence was far too delicate for such undertakings; it was

Thomas who spearheaded our trips (I'd only go when Allen was off somewhere surfing).

Planning our itinerary around a noisy table at The Cave, the *Grapes of Wrath* fantasy was sharing a can of beef stew around a hoboes' campfire, the mournful wail of harmonicas, tales of the Big Strike. The reality turned out to be sharing a bag of Cheetos by the side of a featureless freeway, fearing that we'd be picked up by a knife-wielding maniac, and sleeping in the snow, all of which would have been well-nigh unbearable if we hadn't been wasted almost every minute. We told ourselves, albeit in our cynical, self-mocking way, that we were retracing the steps of Tom Joad and Woody Guthrie, but in fact our trips ended up being one long drunk from beginning to end, highlights of which included a three-day marathon at Tootsie's Orchid Lounge in Nashville, doing Disneyland on LSD, and getting arrested at the Canadian border for possession of amphetamines.

In spite of our mishaps, Tom really was the perfect traveling companion. He wasn't one of those horrible people who want to talk all the time, he turned on the charm to get us free shelter and food, and for someone who would have flunked every institutional leadership exam, he was take-charge, protective, and even chivalrous. He always made sure I got the bigger half of the sandwich, the warmest side of the tent, his extra sweater at night. "Take it. *Take it!*" he'd say, like he was going to beat me up if I didn't.

Once on the Jersey turnpike, we got stuck for hours on an off-ramp. It was the middle of winter: numbingly, whimperingly cold. Finally someone stopped, a VW van. When we climbed in the back and I found out the heater was broken, I almost started crying.

"Take your boots off," Tommy said.

"My feet are *freezing*," I wailed. "Why would I want to take my boots off?"

"Take your boots off!" he said, with his fake mean look.

So I took my boots off, and he dragged me over and unzipped his jacket and took my freezing cold feet and tucked them under his shirt, right against his bare chest. He had to have been at least as cold as I was, and he held my feet, which were like blocks of ice, against his nice warm chest. "I knew Boy Scouts would come in handy for something," he smirked, "even if they did kick me out," and he didn't let go of my feet till they were completely thawed out.

As for the people who picked us up, steelworkers and truck-lift operators were not the type we would take advantage of: it was our peers—granola people, guys in paisley headbands and women in crocheted shawls, anyone who was too earnest or peaceful or non-ironic—whom we had no compunction about milking dry.

One afternoon in rural North Carolina a psychedelic-painted yellow pickup pulled over. At the wheel was a man with a foot-long beard, and in the passenger seat sat a woman in a long gauze dress with a crown of daisies on her head.

"Hello earthlings," she said in the voice of the perpetually stoned.

"Greetings," said the man, the feather in his Robin Hood cap quivering in the breeze. "I'm Pilgrim, and this is my lady, Moon."

Pilgrim and Moon lived on a fifty-acre farm at the end of a long dirt road, and by the time we'd squeezed into the cab, accepted the wineskin of dandelion wine they pressed on us, and given them an embroidered version of our travels— "Cool, man, like blowin' in the wind"—they'd invited us to spend the night. We washed our hands with oatmeal soap, ate cheese made from the milk of goats tethered in the adjacent pasture, and smoked about fifty joints of Pilgrim's home-grown. As we lay on our muslin sheets afterward—Tommy and I routinely undressed in front of one another, slept in the same bed, and curled up together for warmth, all completely platonically—Tommy was so wiped out he even made a move.

"Gross!" I said, slapping away his hand and sending us both into gales of hearty laughter.

The next morning, Moon fed us tea with honey from her hives and biscuits with freshly churned butter. We hung around most of the day reading and resting up, but by dusk we were restless. In his leather jerkin, Pilgrim drove us out to the highway, handed us a bag of hummus sandwiches, and slipped Tom a twenty.

"Go ahead," he said, ducking his head in embarrassment. "It's like it says in *Be Here Now*, gotta give it away to keep it."

"Hey bro, if you're ever in New Hampshire, you have a place to stay," Tommy told him. "No, really, your money's no good there."

"Can't thank you enough," I chimed in, clasping his proffered hand in the hippie handshake.

He pulled away and we watched in silence as his taillights twinkled, grew dim, tapered off.

"What a homo," Tom observed as they disappeared into the dark.

"Totally," I agreed, sticking out my thumb for an oncoming truck. "Hey, where's that twenty? Let's buy a bottle of Jack."

I took the most trips with Thomas, but my longest trip was with Jill. One summer (I think it was the summer before what was supposed to have been my junior year, but by that time I'd taken so many breaks things had gotten a little vague academically) she hooked up with a guy named Chris Reimer, a friend of Billy's who'd flown out from Van Nuys, California, for a few months to work as a volunteer for the Seacoast Anti-Pollution League. "You guys should check out the West Coast," he kept telling us. "There's plenty of room at my parents'."

So that fall, after Chris had left, Jill and I loaded up our backpacks and hitchhiked to California. For reasons I've now forgotten—I think we might have had some harebrained notion of picking fruit in Washington State—we traveled by way of Canada. The way I remember it, Canada was a very large country with not much in it besides the splendid scenery around Banff, and it took what seemed like years to cross it. When we finally arrived, L.A., in spite of the paradisiacal weather, was something of a letdown, too. It was like a giant shopping mall—I had never seen so many cars, people, freeways, or stores—and it dawned on me for the first time in my life that, in its way, New Hampshire was actually kind of pretty. Van Nuys in particular seemed a hideous place (little did I know I would one day make my home within ten miles of it), filled with identical streets of ticky-tacky houses, shaded by identically shaped palm trees, with identical cars parked in the identical driveways.

Culture shock notwithstanding, the Reimers—Chris, his very cute younger brother, and his extremely forbearing parents—couldn't have been nicer or more accommodating: "Hang around for a few months," they urged us. "See how you like it here." So Jill got a job as a receptionist in a dentist's office, and I got a job waitressing at the San Remo Pizza House, feeling sorrier and sorrier for myself by the day, however, because she was *with* her boyfriend and I wasn't. One night, saturated with self-pity, and having downed about a gallon of cheap red wine alone in my bedroom, I decided it was time to leave. (This would become a pattern; over the years I became notorious for my drunken "disappearances.") Scrounging around in my closet, I ripped a flap from a cardboard box, scrawled "East" on it with black Magic Marker, and staggered out to what as nearly as I can figure today must have been Victory Boulevard.

I started to sober up somewhere around Las Vegas ("Whoa, is that all, like, *neon?*") to find myself in the passenger's seat of a tractor trailer driven by a man who, with his lined face, soiled cowboy hat, and ill-fitting toupee, resembled a prematurely aged George Jones. He dropped me off at a truck stop outside Denver, where two refrigerator-sized black guys offered me a lift. As soon as we were on the road, the one in the passenger seat gave me an "Okay, baby, no free rides here" look and jerked his head in the direction of the bed at the back of the cab. "Oh no thank you," I said politely. They kicked me out at the next ramp.

Standing at the exchange of two interstate highways, dirty, tired, hungover, with speeding cars and gigantic semis bearing down on me from every direction and less than ten dollars in my pocket, it came to me that not a soul in the world knew where I was. In a weird way, I *liked* this: the lonelier and more dangerous the situation, the more at home I felt. Still, I wasn't prepared to prostitute myself, or worse, get raped, and I breathed a sigh of relief at my next ride, a retired rodeo rider from Louisiana who was so old and shrunken up he looked like he might blow away in a stiff wind. *Please don't let him ask,* I chanted to myself as I examined his leathery profile, *please don't let him ask.* We rode together for eight hundred miles, eating chicken-fried steak, drinking chemical coffee. Finally, outside of St. Louis, it was time to part ways. He let me off in front of a Kroger's.

"Well, thanks a lot!" I said brightly, reaching for my backpack. "Good luck!"

Just when I thought I was home-free, a scrawny hand clamped down on mine.

"How 'bout it?" he leered. "C'mon, I'll use a *rub*ber." A rubber! As if a *rubber* were the only thing standing in the way!

When I got home I started school again, belatedly got my license, and, with Allen's help, bought my first car, a '62 Impala. My hitchhiking days were over, but the restlessness that lay beneath them was not.

fourteen

Nature—sometimes sears a Sapling—
Sometimes—scalps a Tree—
Her Green People recollect it
When they do not die—

Fainter leaves—to Further Seasons—
Dumbly testify—
We—who have the Souls—
Die oftener—Not so vitally—

—Emily Dickinson

What with falling in love, hitchhiking around the country, and drinking at The Cave, I had to remind myself sometimes that I was still in college. I'd dabbled in philosophy, French, and art history, but the time had come to declare a major. Since the day I'd learned to read, I had known there was only one thing I wanted or was fit to do: write. I talked about writing, I dreamed about writing, I vowed every morning that the next day, without fail, I would begin writing. The only thing I had never done in any sustained, disciplined, focused way was actually write. Fear of failure, fear of success, fear of fulfilling my goal and having nothing left to live for, guilt-driven fear that I didn't deserve to do something that I liked: all these came into play, and they were topped off by a full-blown messiah/martyr complex.

And so, instead of English, the logical choice to launch the career I'd dreamed of since childhood, I chose as my major Social Service—a field in which I didn't have the slightest interest but which I secretly hoped would make people think I was holy. This was a plan that showed immediate signs of failing to pan out, as it was becoming rapidly apparent that I could barely attend to my own needs, never mind those of another bereft soul. I did manage to accompany one poverty-stricken, cancer-ridden woman on the bus to a doctor's appointment at Mass General, where, as we ate lunch in the cafeteria, one of her front teeth fell out in the mashed potatoes—a situation emblematic of so many problems, on so many different levels, that I could think only of my own personal solution to trouble of all kinds and had to restrain myself from grabbing her arm, exclaiming, "You need a drink!" and dragging her off to the nearest bar.

My impulse was good (if a little nebulous)—to help "the poor." I couldn't see how poor *I* was; that by ignoring the call to write I was depriving myself of the best chance I had to help myself. "Ye shall know the truth, and the truth shall set ye free," read the inscription over the entrance to the campus library. The words never failed to stir me, and I pondered them from time to time. Was there even such a thing as truth? What was it? Where did you find it?

I thought the quote was from Abraham Lincoln. I didn't know for a long time afterward it was from the Gospel According to John—that it was something Christ had said to his disciples.

Allen and I had been through a lot together. We'd been to Puerto Rico and Jamaica, we'd been to the wedding of his best friend and the funeral of my grandmother, we'd lived, cooked, laughed, and cried together. And then, when we'd been together four years, we were driving along the beach road one afternoon and he told me that he'd slept with someone else. It was like being kicked in the stomach; I literally couldn't breathe. He had slept with Marty Spodarek, a strapping blond surfer girl who I knew from high school and had always hated; such a *big brazen whore* that she already had an out-of-wedlock baby.

After I'd sobbed and wrung my hands and wailed, "You don't love me anymore! *You. Don't. Love. Me. Any. Mooorrre,*" a couple of hundred times, he dropped me off at my parents' house: they were visiting my mother's relatives in Rhode Island and I was supposed to be babysitting.

Meddy, in third grade by this time, was in the kitchen making cookies. I led her to the right-hand side of the refrigerator, to the cupboard beneath the counter. The vodka was way in the back, between the grapefruit squeezer and the pressure cooker. I told her how to put in a few cubes of ice, fill the glass three-quarters full, and top it off with tomato juice.

"Mostly vodka," I repeated, then went upstairs and crawled into my parents' bed. A couple of minutes later, I opened my eyes to find her standing beside me. "I put some salt and pepper on top," she said anxiously, holding out a triple-strength Bloody Mary. "Is that the way you like it?"

Allen and I saw each other a few more times after that, and though we tried to patch things up, we both knew it was over. "It would be so much better seeing you when possible without giving up other things," he wrote from Sunset Beach, California. "Maybe it is selfish to you, but I've thought about it and at my age and place on the planet it is the way I am. You are really lucky in one way, because you always seem able to ignore everything else but me. You are the one to be hurt when you don't have that one thing, but I can't be happy without doing things on my own too. At least for now . . ."

Someone with a more grounded sense of self might have faced the loss, felt the pain, and worked through to the other side. I pretty much had a nervous breakdown. I stayed drunk for three months. I stopped working, stopped going to school, stopped eating and lost fifteen pounds. I was in the world but not of it; oblivious to whom I talked, what I did, where I stayed; wandering blind in a howling wasteland of grief.

And then one day I came to, and staggered back into the land of the living: blinking my eyes against the light, taking small, uncertain steps. Air seemed miraculous, water, food. After a couple of weeks or so, looking like a concentration camp victim, I felt strong enough to drive to the beach. I drove down by where the surfers were, and parked far enough away so that I wouldn't have to see or talk to any of them. "After great pain, a formal feeling comes— / The Nerves sit ceremonious, like Tombs—" Emily Dickinson wrote. Maybe that's the way, after all this time, I still remember every detail of that day: the wind-whipped waves, the sun-warmed concrete of the seawall, what I was wearing: brown corduroys and an ocean-blue jersey made out of a kind of phosphorescent seventies blend.

Looking out over the water, I spotted him right away, straddling his board. He was only a dot, but I would have known him anywhere. I thought of the shape of his hands, the hollow at the base of his spine, the way my heart had never stopped skipping a beat at the sound of his voice, and I realized it was the kind of loss—because I knew now that the thing I wanted more than anything in the world not to go wrong could—from which I would never fully recover. And I'm not sure I ever fully have.

A few months later, I heard through the grapevine that Allen had married someone else.

fifteen

Those go in disgrace
who carve images.

—Isaiah 45:16

M y concept of love was that it only came once. By some incredible fluke, I had found the one person in the universe meant for me, and now he was gone. I would never have that chance again, I could never go through that kind of pain again, I would never let myself get that close to anyone again. So after the year or so it took me to get over Allen, I determined, when it came to men, to adopt the prevailing wisdom: *I* would be in control! *I* would choose! I wouldn't let them use me; *I* would use *them*!

The problem was that I had an unfortunate tendency to end up actually liking–no matter how low the level of reciprocation–the men I slept with. Thus I wound up with people like Ed, a green-eyed blond in a motorcycle jacket

whose way of introducing himself to a gal was to sneak up
from behind as she was sitting at the bar of The Cave and
grab her breasts. Ed was a mechanic who lived in the woods
outside Durham (personally, I was so uninterested in cars I
didn't even know how to open a hood), the yard of his
A-frame house/body shop strewn with fenders, engine parts,
and a vintage black Jag on concrete blocks.

After a single night together, I of course was wild about
him, but Ed, it soon transpired, was blatantly uninterested in
monogamy, commitment, or even acknowledging me in public, though—after I'd hitchhiked over to see him, often in the
dead of a winter night—he did sometimes condescend to let
me hang around his bachelor pad the next day while he
worked in his shop. As if searching for some stray bit of evidence that I was part of his life, I snooped through his medicine cabinet (tinfoil package of shaving-cream-caked Trojans,
spray can of Kwell), his drawers (odd screws, nude photos of
other girlfriends), his kitchen cupboards (cast-iron frying pan,
chipped Corning Ware casserole), marveling at the very fact
that he existed, that he brushed his teeth and emptied out his
pockets and ate.

When I wasn't snooping, I read, if I'd thought to bring a
book, or stared out the window, or just waited. I waited a lot.
Sometimes one of his friends came by and he and Ed would
stand outside the shop talking, smoking cigarettes, their
laughter drifting upstairs to the living room, where I sat surrounded by the shotgun cabinet, the Johnnie Walker Black
bottle full of pennies, the shelf of Louis L'Amour paperbacks.

If it got to be dinnertime, we rode on his Harley out to the grocery store at the traffic circle and bought a package of chicken thighs, three potatoes—two for him, one for me—and a couple of six-packs. Back at his place, I smeared the chicken with barbecue sauce, pricked the potatoes with a fork, and threw everything in the oven for an hour.

Crazed with loneliness after having spent the entire day by myself, I tried to start a conversation, but Ed had already thrown himself onto his mattress, absorbed in a football game.

"So how'd it go today?" I asked.

"Unh-hunh." Eyes glued to the TV.

"Was that Murph who came by?"

No answer.

I retreated to the kitchen to sip beer and chain-smoke, tracing imaginary pictures on the wood-grain veneer of the dinette table with a dead match, looking out over the tops of the bare trees, shell-shocked by the stupendous gap between bounteous fantasy and meager, meager reality. I spent two years doing that.

After Ed, I gave up all hope and embarked on a rampage of indiscriminate sex (alternating with anorexic, unrequited obsessions) that would last for the remainder of my drinking career, eventually eliminating the need for such time-consuming activities as dating, talking, or learning the other person's name, and also more or less assuring that forever after the subject would be so overlain with guilt, shame, and memories of rejection that twenty years later the wounds are still in the process of healing.

Sexual liberation was great while it lasted, but I'm glad it's over now.

Back then, I didn't need a whole lot of information to make decisions. Are you male? Let's make out. Is it booze? Let's drink it. Lack of instant gratification was one of the reasons (along with the fact that it made me paranoid, and not nearly high enough) that I was never crazy about marijuana: it was just so slooooooow. Some of the most excruciating memories of my early twenties are sitting around while some zoned-out pothead *found* the baggie, and *cleaned* the stemmy wads, and *rolled* the joint, and *looked* for a match, and *took* a hit, and *passed* it on . . . I just wanted to rip the top off a bottle of Mad Dog and start guzzling.

Along the same lines, instead of working and making money and saving up to buy the things I wanted, I often preferred (until I got caught, at which point I was so overcome with shame—as I should have been—that I never did it again) to shoplift. I started out with cosmetics—Yardley lip gloss, Ultralash—branched out to books—the Bhagavad Gita, poetry by Leonard Cohen and Lawrence Ferlinghetti—and moved on to clothes from Spectrum India. When I learned to cook, I started stealing food: capers, Port Salut cheese. From there it was only a short step to Crabtree and Evelyn soap, linen for curtains and tablecloths, even plants. I once stuffed a pot of gloxinia down the back of my jeans and nearly asphyxiated myself in an effort not to have it pop out and crash to the floor as I passed the cash register, expending such a prodigious amount of energy in straining to control my breath, muscles, and mind that I could have gotten a job, earned the money, and opened my own greenhouse.

The irony of instant gratification is that it leaves such lasting scars. I rationalized my stealing with the kind of "they're only capitalist pigs" drivel I was fond of spouting in those days, but even I didn't believe it, and I was only creating more bad karma, only setting myself up for a lifetime of more guilt (not to mention some very mortifying moments of decades-after-the-fact restitution). When I got caught it was for stealing sweaters at the Hayloft, a women's clothing store run by the parents of a town-and-country girl with whom I'd gone to high school. It was mortifying having the whole world know I was a thief: my parents, my classmate, her parents, the kindly Judge Cassasa, who for years had been one of Hampton's two lawyers. A couple of years ago, I sent a letter to Colt's News Store, also a downtown Hampton fixture, enclosing a check for some makeup I'd stolen as a teenager. That summer, home to visit, I stopped into Colt's for a newspaper and ran into Judge Cassasa. "What a nice letter that was!" he said. "Did you know I own Colt's now?"

Today, still trying to prove I'm good, I have to remind myself that it's morally acceptable to own a decent sofa, an appealing car, an item of clothing that's not from the Salvation Army. I've made some progress, but a hundred times a day I still look around my apartment—the secondhand stereo speakers, the yard-sale pillows—and think, See, I'm *not* grabby and greedy! Everything's all right!

sixteen

So we live, forever saying farewell.
        —Rainer Maria Rilke, Eighth Duino Elegy

At the beginning of my last (i.e., seventh) year in college, Tommy rented a place a few miles up Route 108 toward Durham. It was a decrepit farmhouse on a street called Bennett Road, and it was the kind of spot only someone with Tom's unique vision would have taken a second look at. It had exposed beams, pumpkin pine floors, and a claw-footed bathtub, but it also had a caved-in roof, no heat, and, when he first discovered it, no electricity. Like one of those Southwest Native American tribes anthropologists theorize got up from their rabbit and roasted maize one night and vanished into thin air, the former inhabitants of Bennett Road seemed to have fled in the middle of a circa-1942 dinner, leaving behind a complete pigpen. The yard was filled with rusted tractors and plows, the windows were broken, and every room was filled to the ceiling with rubble: bricks, termite-ridden piles of wood, clothes corroded to rags.

"It's a mess!" everyone said.

"It needs a little work," Tommy said, passing another joint. "What are you doing Saturday?"

Tom was nothing if not persuasive, and using massive amounts of marijuana and beer as a lure—"Keep the buzz going" was his mantra—that winter he commandeered the help of family and friends and transformed Bennett Road into an actual place to live. People drywalled and painted, swept and scrubbed, hauled load after load to the dump. "It's all comin' together," Tom bobbed his head knowingly, unloading a secondhand woodstove from his truck with one hand and taking a hit off his ubiquitous spliff with the other. It's a wonder nobody nailed their fingers to a board or fell off the roof, but by spring Tommy, his dog Lout, and what quickly became a rotating group of anywhere from four to ten people were ready to move in.

That summer he cajoled a neighboring farmer into lending him a backhoe, put in a vegetable garden, and doled out tomatoes, cucumbers, and zucchini whenever Terry or I came by. One night a bunch of us were hanging around in the front yard drinking beer when Thomas had yet another of his brainstorms.

"Hey, I know, let's have a clambake," he said. "It'll be like a housewarming. We'll invite our parents and shit."

"Yeah, let's have a clambake," Johnnie Hayes chimed in, draining his twentieth or so Bud. "At the company picnic they line a bunch of garbage cans with seaweed, and then they put lobsters and potatoes and corn in old pillowcases . . ."

"No way," Tom interrupted, licking the seam of a cigar-sized joint. "The way the Indians did it, they dug a hole and got the coals going and put everything right in the ground."

"Could be kind of tricky," Terry observed. "If the coals don't get hot enough . . ."

"Chick will help," Tom said, waving an expansive hand. Chick was an old guy from the Legion who rode around town on a beat-up Schwinn, trolled the local river for fish, and had a speech impediment that made him barely intelligible to the uninitiated. "Mmmnmm, hnmmmmm, *nmnnnnn*," Chick would say, and when you said "Hunh?" Tommy would translate, "Oh, he says the smelt are running down at the weirs again."

So we set a date, pitched in forty bucks apiece, and invited our parents and friends, everyone from The Cave, and half the remaining residents of Newmarket and Durham. The day before the party, some of us went down to the beach and gathered buckets of seaweed, some of us went to buy lobster and corn and beer, and some of us dug a giant hole in the ground, lined it with rocks and wood, and got a fire going. Chick rode his bike up from Newmarket and supervised, with instructions only Tommy could understand.

That night we all slept over at Bennett Road. The clam-bake was scheduled to start at two, but unfortunately we'd stayed up so late the night before getting loaded that nobody came to till around ten, by which time the fire, which was sup-posed to have been smoldering all night, was completely dead.

"Torch it up," Tom said, his hand on a stone-cold rock. "Who's got the weed?"

We piled on enough wood to start a bonfire and doused it with gasoline, but when Chick dropped by at eleven, he surveyed the scene, cast a mournful look Tommy's way, and sadly shook his head. At noon, in strained silence, we threw on three hundred dollars' (1977 dollars) worth of lobsters, a hundred and fifty of clams, dozens of hot dogs, and half an acre's yield of corn on the cob.

"Keep the buzz going," said Tom. "Who wants to make a beer run?"

Promptly at two my parents made their way up the driveway. Mom was toting a casserole dish of paprika-sprinkled potato salad, and Dad sported a new Greek fisherman's cap for the occasion. "Hi Mom, hi Dad," I said brightly. "The lobsters should be ready any minute."

"Oh, you're cooking them on coals?" my father asked. "The way we always do it at the boat club, we get a few garbage cans and some old pillowcases . . ."

People were coming in droves now, bringing cases of beer, more hot dogs, tomatoes from their gardens. Tom stumbled over, his eyes bloodshot. "Want some chips, Mrs. King?" he leered, brandishing a sodden bag of Lay's. "Al! Have a Bud!"

We prodded the lobsters and turned the lobsters and put more fire on the lobsters, and at five the lobsters were still half raw, the clams tightly shut, the potatoes as hard as the rocks they were supposed to have been cooking on.

"That was fun, Heath," Mom said graciously as my parents took their leave, and Dad said, "Plenty of beer, anyway. Come on down to the house for dinner soon."

The others were drifting home, too. By seven, it was just Terry, Tommy, Hayes, and me, along with a mountain of empty beer cans and a hole in the ground with about eighty inedible lobsters in it.

Tommy would go on to break many hearts, father three children, and die at the age of forty-one after drinking so much alcohol and doing so many drugs that his body simply shut down. I like to remember him as he was that night, though, still in his prime.

"It's all comin' together now," he said with a contented smile. "Who's driving to The Cave?"

I graduated that fall, three and a half years late. I'd been eligible for Phi Beta Kappa, but blew it at the last minute with an incomplete in Advanced Statistics: one of the few times I had ever seen my mother on the verge of tears. Part of me wanted to ask, "What's *wrong* with me?" and part of her probably wanted to say something, too, but neither of us did. I think we both knew by that time I was never going to use my degree. If there was one thing college had proved, it was that I wasn't shaping up to be nine-to-five material.

seventeen

O Lord I have loved the beauty of thy house,
and the place where thy glory dwelleth.

—Psalm 26

Terrence had started dating a nice boy named Stephen, an artist from Nashville who'd been living in Boston for a couple of years. When Terry suggested that *we* move to Boston, I jumped at the chance. I'd long ago worn out my welcome in Newmarket, and what with my burgeoning drinking-and-driving problem, a subway system sounded like an excellent idea. Museums, theaters, fine food: my brain raced with the possibilities. Having long known that my unique talents were going unrecognized in the New Hampshire backwoods, it was thrilling to think of a new canvas on which to paint my delightful, colorful self.

Steve lived in a loft in the old West End, so Terry and I rented an apartment in nearby Beacon Hill. 37 Anderson

Street (I once emerged from a blackout to find myself in a vacant studio with my head covered in blood, stumbled outside,
and, after wandering blindly around for half an hour, realized
I'd somehow found my way to 37 *Garden* Street, one block
west of our own abode) was a space that managed to cram a
kitchen, a bathroom, and what was advertised as two bed-
rooms into approximately 350 square feet. The front (only)
door opened directly into the first bedroom (view of airless
shaft), which proceeded into the bathtub-sized living room
(view of dungeon-like "courtyard"), a kitchen so small one
had to stand in the hallway in order to open the refrigerator,
and a second "bedroom" that was barely bigger than one of
those cabinets they used to store ironing boards in.

It soon transpired as well that the entire apartment was
overrun with cockroaches. In my naïveté, I at first assumed
that all city residences were thus infested, but in twenty-five
years of urban living since, never have I seen anything remotely approaching a similar concentration of vermin. Not
only were the usual places like the kitchen sink, the cof-
feemaker, and the toothbrush holder swarming with repul-
sively capsule-like brown bodies; armies of the loathsome
creatures had also set up camp in dresser drawers, lamp
shades, and pillowcases. I'd be donning my favorite sweater
and a battalion of cockroaches would shower from the neck.
Terr would go to look up that Frank O'Hara poem we loved
about Billie Holiday, and the page would be covered with the
dry, sepia-colored husks of dead cockroaches.

Luckily, none of this bothered me much, as my first night
in town, I'd walked up Cambridge Street—past Jobi's Liquor,

the Lamplighter Laundromat, and the Red Hat—wandered around a corner, and discovered Misty's. Misty's was your quintessential working-class Boston dive—Schlitz mirrors, Bruins pennants, black plastic ashtrays overflowing with butts. That would have been attraction enough, but it also happened to have been Thursday and the bouncer was handing out little yellow cards reading "Ladies Night! Twenty-five-cent cocktails!" I introduced myself to the bartender, made friends with two cab drivers, and got bombed for less than ten bucks. By last call, museums, theaters, and fine food had all gone out the window in favor of drinking myself into a nightly stupor in this dank, airless hole.

The bar upon which *Cheers* was based was mere blocks away, but Misty's had nothing to recommend it to the tourist, and the regulars bore no resemblance to the lovable characters presided over by Ted Danson. In fact, most of them could barely hold a conversation, never mind engage in the sustained give-and-take required for, say, a two-minute TV skit. Ray the Bookie, a sixty-three-year-old cokehead, droned endlessly on about eight-balls, baby powder, and Maalox. Jo-Jo, a low-level mafioso who was reputed to have been hit over the head with a baseball bat, responded to all attempts at communication—How 'bout them Celts? Where's the bartender?—with a single sentence: "Go shit in your hat." Edie, a junkie from the Charlestown projects, nodded off over her 7-and-7's for so long that we sometimes took the cigarette from her hand so she wouldn't burn her fingers.

By this time, I'd hit upon a winning social strategy: find a group of people with whom I had nothing in common, and who held me in complete contempt, and make every effort to spend eight to ten hours a day with them. The bartenders at Misty's fit the bill perfectly. A tightly knit gang of Irish Catholics from working-class "Dohchestah," they wore Claddagh rings on their wedding-band fingers and gold chains around their bull-like necks. They smoothed back their hair and checked out their profiles in the mirror behind the bar. They were sexist, racist, and homophobic, and they looked like they mainlined steroids. Patrick had a chest like the prow of a ship and drove a black Coupe de Ville with plates that read "BUFF." Tony had hands like waffle irons and was engaged to a manicurist. Kieran had biceps the size of breadfruits and aspired to open a tire shop. They had no use whatsoever for someone whose main outside interest was reading, and it hardly raised their opinion of me that I eventually slept with most of them.

Terrence—who had started to hang out at gay bars like the Ramrod Room and Buddy's—was (rightfully) appalled. "Oh, it's kind of a hoot," I told him, not knowing that the hoot would last eight years and that I would blow so much money on drinks, tipping the insolent bartenders, and cab fare to and from Misty's that I could have purchased a mansion on the coast of Maine, a small yacht, or an annuity that would have supported me well into my dotage—assuming I lasted that long, which by that time was starting to look extremely doubtful.

Deep in my heart, I knew how pathetic it was to be spending so much time in a sleazy bar, how embarrassing it was to be hanging out with people who didn't even like me, how helpless I was to leave. I'd lost my old support system and, with my niggardly, one-chance worldview, in this new place I felt like I had to settle for whoever would have me. Things would be different in Boston, I'd told myself. Coming to one morning after I'd been there a few months, I gazed out, hungover, at the drab brick wall outside my bedroom window and realized they *were* different. They were worse.

In spite of my drinking, Boston really was a wondrous city, and Terry was the ideal person with whom to explore it. We walked through the streets pushing, shoving, goosing each other; enjoying a moment of silence as we stood on the Longfellow Bridge and gazed at the sunlight sparkling on the Charles, or perused the menu in the window of a Back Bay restaurant that was far beyond our means. He might put a tenderly restraining hand on my shoulder as I was about to dash, unheeding, into traffic; or we'd be walking through the Public Garden, gawking at the pink-and-white blossoms of what we called "tulip trees," and suddenly I'd feel an arm gripping me tight and a large face shoved into mine saying, "Heather. King! I. Love. *You!*"

It wasn't that Terry and I would have had the perfect relationship except for the fact that we didn't have sex; given the circumstances, it *was* the perfect relationship because it was emotional and even physical without the slightest bit of sexual tension. In public, we often pretended to make out, inserting a thumb between our mouths as we moaned and writhed, and we were privy to the most intimate details of each other's love lives, bodily functions ("How's your period, hon?" "Oh my God, let me see, is that *herpes*?"), and existential fears and sorrows.

When I was hungover, he lay beside me in bed and read me poetry: Yeats's "When you are old and gray / And sitting by the fire . . ."; Auden's "Lay your sleeping head, my love, human on my faithless arm . . ." On our days off, we took the subway to Copley Square and, in the central courtyard of the public library, sat in black Windsor chairs and smoked and read, with a square of cloudy gray sky overhead and stone urns of geraniums lining the gravel paths.

Terr had Stephen now, though, and I needed a new friend, too. This turned out to be Dot, the only woman I knew who spent more time at Misty's than I did—mainly because, as the sole female bartender, she worked there. The two of us sat by the hour: gossiping, character assassinating, critiquing but secretly lusting after the bartenders. Kieran, due to the optical illusion created by his bulked-out shoulders, we referred to (privately of course) as Pinhead. Tony, another Schwarzenegger lookalike, was Ape; Finn, barely ten pounds overweight, Sperm Whale. This might have been mean, except that they couldn't have cared less what we thought, and paid not the slightest attention to us.

Though she barely ate enough to keep a bird alive, Dot was often on a diet herself, and she had some novel ideas about exercise. One was that playing pinball burned off calories: "It's cardiovascular," she explained, shifting the machine with a dainty hip. Another was that smoking only enhanced the effects of a good workout. One afternoon I dropped by her apartment. "Whip It" blared from the tape deck, a bag of Doritos gaped open on the coffee table, and Dot lay on the rug, one hand propping up her head, the other holding a Marlboro 100. "I'm doing leg lifts," she explained, taking a leisurely drag. Which, for that matter, was more exercise than I ever did.

Sylvia, an Italian beautician in her early fifties, was one of the more raucous of the Misty's regulars—her Saturday night entrance consisted of strolling in with her poodle, Princess, standing stock still, and yelling down the length of the bar, "Anyone get *laid* this week?"—but she was also responsible and mature in a way that put the rest of us to shame. For Superbowl Sunday, she spent days ahead of time cooking giant pans of lasagna and ziti with meatballs, then hauled them down to the bar from her apartment. She took in her nephew Bruce—who'd done one too many hits of acid in high school and hadn't been right since—when her sister found him too much to handle, brought her wheelchair-bound father to Mass every Sunday, and many nights dragged me back to her apartment after the bar closed, warmed up a bowl of *pasta e fagioli*, and put me to bed on her couch.

In between, she worked six days a week at Shear Magic, her downtown hair salon, which was located on the second floor of a Winter Street merchant's building. One Saturday afternoon on my way home from Filene's, I walked up a creaking set of wooden stairs and down a hallway filled with driving schools and cut-rate travel agents and stopped in for a visit. Bruce lounged slack-jawed in a chair of turquoise vinyl, Princess dozed by the utility tray, and smoke from Sylvia's

Virginia Slim, perched in its glass ashtray, wafted over a sink full of pink foam curlers.

"Heathah! Come in, come in, whadja buy, ya hungry?" Sylvia yelled, waving a hand whose fingers gripped little rectangles of white tissue paper. "She's hungry, Bruce, run down to Bailey's and get her a turkey sandwich, she likes lettuce, take it out of my wallet."

"No, Syl–" I started to say.

"Fuhgedabout it. Buy me a drink next time if you want."

I made myself at home, spreading out on an orange recliner, lighting my own cigarette, and surveying the scene. One woman was reading *Ladies' Home Journal* under the clear plastic bonnet of a hair dryer; another, a hefty gal in knee-length Supp-Hose, stared stolidly ahead as gray goo dripped down her thinning scalp. Sylvia was short and curvy, with oversized glasses that made her look slightly bug-eyed, and she had the easy economy of movement that comes from years of practicing the same trade in the same small space. Moving between the sink, the supply closet, the three Naugahyde chairs, she kept up a running patter. "Too hot, Gert, turn it down, no, no, hon, on the right, like that." "Lo, fifteen minutes, you want another magazine?" "Is that Patrick cute down the bah, Heathah? Twenty yeahs youngah and I'd jump his bones . . ."

I'd only planned on staying a couple of minutes, but the conversation–the latest Kennedy scandal, the bum of a mayor, the son who was going to be a cop–was as soothing as the sound of a Red Sox game coming over the radio on a summer's day. "Can you believe the price of bedspreads,

Sylvia? Fohty dollahs for a twin," Lo shook her head, and Gert weighed in with, "Three-fifty now they want in the bakery for a dozen macaroons!" More clients drifted in, women who had been coming to Sylvia for twenty or thirty years, who worked as housekeepers or nannies, and shopped the sales at Jordan Marsh, and had grown children who didn't pay enough attention to them. Sylvia called them "deah" and treated them like angels, as if they had glorious manes of golden tresses and had floated up the stairs on wings instead of hauling their swollen carcasses one step at a time, stopping to shift their bags and catch their breath.

I ate my sandwich and shot the breeze with Bruce—"Bruce, dja get bombed last night?": "Unh, yuh"; "Bruce, how much ya smokin' these days?": "Two packs, Syl's gonna kill me"— and finally it was time to leave: I had to get ready for work. "Thanks, Syl, so long, Bruce," I said, gathering up my things.

"Take this shampoo, Heathah, it's a sample," Sylvia said, handing me a full-sized bottle of Pantene. "Brucie, wrap up those chocolates for her, we'll never eat them all." She was combing out and spraying one of her clients, an exhausted-looking soul with an Ace bandage wrapped around her elbow who left just before me. I trailed the woman downstairs. Just before hitting the street she paused to girlishly admire, in the reflection of the plate-glass door, her shapeless coat and work-worn face topped by a spun-glass halo of bright, pretty hair.

There was something different about Sylvia, something I couldn't quite put my finger on at the time. Unlike me, she didn't live entirely for herself.

eighteen

In vain your earlier rising,
Your going later to rest,
You who toil for the bread you eat:
While he pours gifts on his beloved while
    they slumber.

—Psalm 27

S hortly after moving to town, Terry and I both got jobs waiting tables. His was at Lombardo's, a popular family-style
restaurant in the Italian North End. I was working at a good-
sized seafood place near Somerville's Davis Square (a terrible
commute necessitating a subway ride across the Charles River
followed by a half-mile walk) called Cherrystones.

Cherrystones' no-frills, what-you-see-is-what-you-get approach had garnered it a loyal local following and made it a
favorite with tourists as well. The menu was printed daily on
a chalkboard, customers ate cheek-by-jowl with strangers at
cafeteria tables, and, instead of having designated stations,

the waitstaff circulated around getting drinks for, answering
the questions of, and delivering food to whoever flagged us
down (we pooled our tips). Partly because it really was kind
of fun, partly because I was usually at least half in the bag, I
wasn't quite as abusive to my customers as usual. Well into
the spirit of the thing, they stared hungrily at my hustled-by
plates—"Is that monkfish?" "Are those *raw*?"—and good-
naturedly righted themselves as I plowed into their chairs.
Whipping this daily dog-and-pony show into shape was the
militant but motherly head waitress, Rose. All the customers
adored her and slavishly awaited her commands, which were
issued in a brisk, come-now-let's-all-do-our-parts Irish brogue.

Even with twenty-five years of hindsight, I have to say the
people who owned this place were not my all-time favorite
bosses, but then again, I was hardly the ideal employee. Far
from being grateful that, in my condition, I'd been hired for
any position above floor-scrubber, my attitude was that they
were lucky to have me: one, because someone of my towering intellect was condescending to waitress at all; and two, because I was usually so hungover I belonged in a hospital.

To that end, I liked to consider the restaurant an extension of my own home; what with the four or five drinks I enjoyed at Misty's each afternoon before coming in, the amount
of time I spent there pulling double shifts to meet my consid-
erable expenses, and my eating and drinking habits while on
duty, it might as well have been. The first thing I did after
punching in, for example, was manufacture an excuse to
head to the walk-in—"*I'll* restock the butter pats!"—and cram
my apron pockets full of jumbo cocktail shrimp. Nothing

made me happier than toting around twenty bucks' worth of
linty, contraband shellfish: it was right in line with my view of
a universe in which there was never enough—food, money,
love—and that had to be cheated into coughing up more. I
then positioned paper soufflé cups of cocktail sauce and blue-
cheese dressing all around the dining room—the edge of the
salad bar, behind the coffee machine—so that, whenever the
spirit moved me, I could dart my hand into my pocket, dip a
crustacean into the appropriate condiment, and scarf it down.
One of my other tricks was filching food from customers'
plates as they sat under the heat lamp: I'd palm, say, a fried
oyster and, covering my mouth in a fake cough, catapult it
down practically whole. Germs meant nothing to me, and I
was by no means above rooting around in the bus bucket if
an especially choice morsel caught my eye. The owner once
yelled at me for chewing gum; I didn't have the heart to tell
him my mouth was full of broiled lobster. They fed us at the
end of the night—mussels steamed in beer, chunks of halibut—
but I was too stuffed from my cloak-and-dagger scavenging
by that time to enjoy it.

When it came to uniforms, everyone was assigned a lame-
ass blue apron—the bib emblazoned with a logo of a fat-
lipped, jokester-looking clam—and girls had to wear skirts,
but other than that we were pretty much on our own. I was
partial to two scoop-necked T-shirts—one bluish-green, one
apricot—very tight, that showed my cleavage: there was no
telling when some good-looking guy with a hankering for
haddock might wander in. The restaurant's best feature,
however, I soon discovered, was that while cocktails and

good wine had to be ordered from the upstairs bar, table wine was stored in green-glassed gallon bottles in the takeout-room fridge, and we got to pour it ourselves. At the first twinge of despair, fatigue, or existential nausea, I learned to head back there, fill a paper cup to the brim, and drain it in a single gulp. After a few of those metallic blasting interludes, even the busiest shift seemed more bearable.

When I wasn't drinking, eating purloined food, or scoping the dining room for guys, I was sneaking out back to the fish-cutters' restroom for a smoke. Ignoring the dirty work clothes heaped on the floor—cotton pants in a hound's-tooth check, white shirts stained with fish blood—I'd light a Winston, flick my ashes in the sink, check my mascara, and calculate how many hours it would be before I was back at Misty's. It smelled like a sewer in there but, perched on the edge of the toilet seat, at least I could rest for a minute. Stealthily emerging one night, I looked both ways to make sure nobody was looking, made a beeline for the telephone cubicle that was supposed to be reserved for credit-card-approval calls, and rang Terrence at Lombardo's to firm up our drinking plans for later. "God this place sucks," I sighed, reaching into my pocket for another jumbo shrimp. "Everyone is so *lazy*."

Actually I felt deeply affectionate toward most of my co-workers, probably in somewhat the same way, and for the same reason, that soldiers in trenches feel affection for their fellow soldiers. My best friend at work was Leonard, who was gay and one of the few people I have ever met about whom I can say with confidence that he was a worse drunk than me.

At twenty-nine, he had the caved-in chest and eggplant-colored nose of a seasoned sot, and we often spent our lunch break downing shots of Wild Turkey at a jazz joint-by-night dive up the street. Leonard's favorite saying was "God love ye," which he'd picked up from Rose. "Be off with ye now, hon, and fetch me a calamari cocktail," he'd giggle in a fake brogue, lurching past with a plate of fried smelts on either arm, his breath trailing the scent of Manhattans. He had a sister named Pixie, also a giant lush, who sometimes joined us after work, and by the end of a typical night the two of them would all but have to be carried out of the bar on gurneys.

Other core members of the waitstaff included Wanda, a pathological liar whose husband, José, the rest of us were convinced was a figment of her imagination; Fritz, who had a nasty habit of always leaving the chowder pot empty; and Irene, a piano student who we all felt protective toward because her mother had committed suicide by drinking Drano. Waiting for the dinner rush to begin, we'd settle into a table in the takeout room, get a big gray tub of silverware from the dishwashers, and start filling the white wax-paper bags—fork, knife, spoon, twist, toss—we carried around in our apron pockets to slap down in front of new customers. Drinking coffee, smoking cigarettes, bitching and gossiping: this was where we really bonded. If nobody was on a diet that day, we'd kick in and someone would run to the dessert place next door for paper plates of chocolate espresso cake or apple crisp with cinnamon ice cream. "Come now, girrrrls, put that away," Rose would dash in and scold when it started to get busy, and we were off like shots.

Stanley, the owner's nephew, was our boss, but we really worked for Rose. Not only because she was on the floor every second working with us, but because she was far and away the only person in management who generated our devotion and respect. Rose had come over from Ireland twenty years before and been employed at Cherrystones ever since. She had iron-gray, tightly permed hair with Mamie Eisenhower bangs, milky skin overlain with a thin sheen of perspiration, and piercing—*piercing!*—blue eyes. Sturdy, a little thick around the waist, she wore polyester dresses in flower prints and spotless white shoes, and she was probably the hardest-working person I have ever met in my life. I mean she *slaved* for those people: twelve, sixteen hours a day; six, seven days a week. She was a whirlwind: patting, prodding, poking, egging us on to work harder, move faster, make more money for the already filthy-rich owners, and all the time she was working herself: taking orders, delivering food, hustling upstairs to the bar. "Be off with ye now, hon, table four at the end," she'd say, cramming a plate of calamari into your hand, or "The nice gentleman with the green tie, ask him if he wants dessert, he's a friend of Stanley's," shooing you off with a little pat on the ass.

Rose's fairness was extra welcome because the other people we had to deal with were so mean. Stanley had all the personal warmth of a snake. Doris, the cashier, possessed the black under-eye circles of a person who stays up nights scheming new ways to be needlessly difficult, unpleasant, and unaccommodating. Carl, the head cook, had beady eyes behind Coke-bottle glasses, dyed auburn locks covered with a

hairnet, and the bad-nerves physique of a pipe-cleaner. Carl
was in the throes of a perpetual hissy fit. He had one of those
bells you see on the desks of hotel clerks in old movies, and
whenever a plate of food was ready you'd hear, Ding! Ding,
ding, ding, ding, *ding!* He'd stand there, hands on either side
of his waist, just waiting for you to show up so he could say,
"It's about time. What ah youse girls, out theah puttin' on ya
eyelinah?"

Between the main dining room and the takeout counter
was the fish market, where we ordered oysters, cherrystones,
and sashimi. One Portuguese fish cutter, Manny, who was
thickset and ponderously slow and spoke about three words
of English, I latched on to right away. "Manny, Manny!" I'd
wave, sprinting through with a gallon plastic container of tartar sauce, and he'd look up from the slab of salmon he was
working on, and his eyes would light up, and he'd smile that
beatific smile of his that lifted my heart. Who needs words to
say "Are you holding up okay?" "Only three more hours; we
can do it." "I'm glad you're here." Those were the moments
that got me through the night; in the restaurant business, you
need all the allies you can get.

I might have slightly overestimated my own contribution, but
we really did work our asses off. It wasn't just waiting on
people—taking orders, running upstairs for drinks, delivering
food, adding checks, bringing them up to the register. It was
making coffee, bringing out more chowder, stocking the
rolls, the butter, the creamers, tea bags, coffee filters, salad
dressing—French, Russian, Italian, blue cheese. Lettuce, toma-

toes, cucumber, sliced red onion we brought out in giant aluminum bins. Cocktail sauce, cocktail forks, cups, soufflé cups, paper cups for iced tea and coffee, saucers, dessert plates, something was always running out or needing to be cleaned up: Ding! Ding, ding, ding, ding, *ding*! Steamers were served in red-and-white cardboard trays, with clam broth and extra butter, and the customers would make a mess and want more napkins and you'd have to wipe it all up before serving the entrée.

Rainbow trout you had to fillet at the table: whip out one of your bags of silverware, extract the knife, cut off the head and tail, slice it down the middle, peel back the halves, zip out the bone: "Ooh, aah, isn't that wonderful?" they'd say, and you'd answer, "Yes, isn't it?"–Ding! Ding, ding, ding, ding, *ding*! A boiled lobster, which meant more melted butter, an extra cardboard tray with a pair of lobster crackers, a pick for the claw meat, and a plastic lobster bib, which you were supposed to tie around the person's neck as if they were handless. "There you go"–*Ding*! Crash! "We're all out of bread plates!" someone would yell, as Rose rushed by to ask, "Can ye work for me Sunday? I know ye've not had a day off this week, but we're verrrry short, and Stanley . . ." Was it any wonder I drank? I asked myself.

Actually, I'm pretty sure Rose knew I drank; that when Leonard and I took off on our lunch hour, we weren't going to the Athenaeum. When we came back, I sometimes caught her staring at me for a second too long with those all-seeing eyes. If Stanley was around, she'd shoot me a "Watch your mouth, now" look, but, bless her Irish heart, she never said a word.

When I thought about it—and I stayed drunk enough so I didn't think about it much—I told myself my life was temporarily on hold while I figured out what to do. That was all. I was just figuring out what to do.

But inside, when I woke up in the morning and dragged myself to the Hilltop Market for a donut and coffee, I was starting to get scared; I was starting to think, This is awful. I keep thinking things are going to change but they never do. I keep thinking I'm going to write but I never do. I keep telling myself I'll find a nice guy—soon—but I never do.

Could my drinking be a . . . problem?

nineteen

For the good that I will to do, I do not do; but
the evil I will not to do, that I practice.
　　　　　　　　　　　—St. Paul, Romans 7:19

After we'd lived at Anderson Street for a year or so, Terry decided he'd move in over with Stephen at his loft. Typically thoughtful, before leaving he procured me a new roommate: a fellow waiter from Lombardo's named Albert. Albert was tall and willowy, with a Beatles mop top, Mick Jagger lips, and hands and feet that were lavender from poor circulation. This last could have had something to do with his nicotine addiction: every time I turned around, he was taking a cheeks-sucked-in drag off a butt, exhaling a mushroom cloud of smoke, and tapping the resulting half-inch of ash into a dirty coffee mug. Albert slept twelve hours a day, spent an hour and a half blow-drying his hair, and the rest of the time worked (a born waiter, he loved his job), swilled booze, and cruised the bars for guys. He went for the smaller types, and for a while there, every time I entered or exited the apartment, I would have to step over a fragile-looking fellow sitting in Albert's dimly lit bedroom, smoking a cigarette in his bathrobe and watching cartoons.

By this time I myself had discovered the morning drink, and was blacking out almost every night. Perhaps a word is in order on the subject of blackouts. When I say blacked out, I mean that from somewhere around ten o'clock at night until one or two or three or whatever time I rolled home the next morning (I would know, if at all, only from asking Dot the next day), I would not remember where I was, what I had done or said, or whom I was with. I routinely had arguments with, made plans concerning, and told the story of my life to people of whom I had no recollection whatsoever. "You're just going to pretend nothing happened?" "Where were you yesterday afternoon?" and "You told me that last night, remember?" were questions I heard frequently.

One night at work I was suddenly struck with a recollection of having had a long telephone conversation a couple of evenings before with Dianne DeMink, a friend from New Hampshire. Dianne had a huge heart, and I didn't know if I was dreaming, but the phrases "volunteered to cook," "fifty-person dinner," and "homeless shelter" kept coming up. Those were in her voice; as I dug deeper into my memory bank, the phrase that kept coming up in mine was "love to help." Then I remembered that my telephone (this was in the days before answering machines) had started ringing around two that afternoon and hadn't stopped till four when I'd left to go to work. That weekend she called, furious. "Why did you tell me you were going to show up if you weren't? I would have asked somebody else! I had to cook that whole dinner by myself!" I was too embarrassed to tell her I'd barely remembered the conversation and had been too hung-over to even answer a telephone, much less take a bus to New Hampshire and/or cook.

Naturally this kind of behavior also led to some very awkward situations that involved waking up in strange beds. "What's the matter?" a man I had never to my knowledge seen before would leer, "You weren't so shy last night." At which point I'd jump up, dress, and flee in horror only to get out on the street and realize I had no idea what part of town I was in. I'd stumble around till I found the nearest subway station, take the Orange Line or the Green Line to the Red Line, get off at Charles Station, then slink down Cambridge Street and up Anderson to home, a route I referred to as the walk of shame.

One reason I blacked out was that I drank so much, and another was that I drank really, really fast. When I walked into a bar "sober," for example (I was never really sober, but when my blood alcohol level dropped down to, say, 0.5 instead of the usual 3.0 or 4.0), the utter inanity of my life in general, and Misty's (or whatever other dive I'd wandered into) in particular, were borne in upon me with such painful clarity that I'd be forced to swill down four or five drinks within the first half hour. (Eventually, in fact, I found it so difficult to endure the schlocky decor, imbecilic conversation, and my own toadying behavior toward the bartenders for even thirty minutes that I took to "bracing up" at home *before*

I went out to Misty's.) This was the half hour I lived for, when all was suffused with a rosy glow, and I felt nothing but magnanimity toward my fellow man and even (completely inappropriately) myself. Typical thoughts during this stage (without fail entirely untrue) included, "I can do it tomorrow"; "They won't mind if I call in sick"; and, unwaveringly disastrous, "I think he likes me."

Regrettably, this all-too-small window of well-being would segue almost directly into oblivion, an often volatile transition since I was also a Dr. Jekyll–and–Mr. Hyde, mean drunk. "You are *sooo* great," I'd divulge impulsively in the early part of the evening, hangdog eyes brimming with affection. The very next instant, unbeknownst to you, your depths would suddenly be revealed to me: I would see that you were petty, grasping, revoltingly egotistical (never realizing that this was in fact a description of myself). With "You are *sooo* great" still ringing in your ears, I'd turn to light a cigarette, swing back, and, seemingly out of the blue, slur, "You suuuuuuuck." Then I'd wonder why I never had a boyfriend.

Beyond sporadic efforts to "pace" myself, I never much tried to control my drinking. I'd go through phases—shots of tequila, Bombay martinis—but the result was always the same, and it never for a minute occurred to me to not drink at all. Terrence and I were always going out for expensive baked stuffed lobster dinners at Dini's or the Union Oyster House and thinking it was just a riot that, between the predinner cocktails, and the wine, and the coffees with Grand Marnier, the bar bill was even higher than the food. But pretty quickly, my tastes got much more plebeian. I drank rivers of a cloying brew called Almaden Mountain White Chablis—whose chief attributes were that it was sold at the local Stop and Shop and cost only $2.39 a half gallon—and once startled an extremely rare "date" (I didn't date, I just turned to whoever was sitting next to me at last call and asked if he wanted to come home with me) who'd brought along a bottle of wine by not only downing his solo, but then whipping my own out of my purse and drinking that, too. I drank beer if there was nothing else on hand, but considered it too weak to be a real drink and only drank more later to make up for it, and the more I drank, the thirstier I seemed to get.

Basically, I'd drink anything, in any mixture and any quantity—my rusty nail, your leftover sombrero; I had an iron stomach and very rarely threw up—but, like many alcoholics, I eventually settled upon vodka as my drink of choice. It went down easy, it was cheap, and I became especially partial to the gimlet—vodka in a rocks glass with ice and a few drops of lime juice: not because I particularly liked the taste, but because it was almost 100 percent pure booze.

Naturally all of this led to daily, excruciating hangovers. The worst of these wasn't the throbbing brain, the smoldering breath, the sweating from every pore of what felt like formaldehyde; it was the overwhelming sense of impending doom, the head-in-one's-shaking-hands feeling of being alone in an alien universe. The only cure seemed to be to start drinking again, and as my hangovers gradually got worse, "cocktail hour" gradually inched forward from five to two to eleven to nine to the minute I got up in the morning. It would

be a few years before I became a round-the-clock maintenance drinker, but already I thought nothing of starting my
day with a half pint of gin, or a couple of rum-and-OJ's.

Every once in a while I'd resolve to go on the wagon, but
this never lasted very long. Once, after a particularly vicious
bender, I ended up at Mass General with strep throat and a
finger I vaguely remembered having slashed on a bottle and
that needed stitches. That's it, I thought, I have *got* to cut
down. Partly because I was too sick and partly because for
once in my life I didn't really want to, I didn't have a drink
for two days. By day three, I was up and about, feeling like a
million bucks. By day four, I was gabbing on the phone, making plans. On day five, I took a long walk along the Charles,
had my hair cut, and made a dentist's appointment. On day
six, I didn't think, Oh I feel so good when I'm not drinking,
I'm never going to drink again! I thought, Oh good, I can
control my drinking like a normal person; I think I'll have a
drink!

In fact, I had several; off and running before the night was
out on yet another bender. It was as if the part of my brain
that governed experience had been lobotomized, and this
sense of being so deeply separated from my truest, sanest
self—the fact that on the one hand I felt *compelled* to engage in
behavior that basically consisted of doing the same thing over
and over again and expecting different results, and that on
the other hand I was somehow *willing* it—created a moral/psy-
chic conflict of such ghastly proportions and satanic complexity I simply tuned it out. Unable to reconcile my warring
parts, I stuffed my feelings, tamped down every uncomfort-

able emotion, compartmentalized myself into two different people—good versus bad, self-pitying versus compassionate, sarcastic versus thoughtful—never knowing who I was, or able to predict who I was going to be, on any given occasion. And then I had another drink.

With this self-sabotaging lifestyle, perhaps it was no surprise that anyone twisted, dark, and sick I was attracted to, and anyone healthy and sane I avoided like the plague. One afternoon in the fiction stacks at the library a perfectly pleasant, nice-looking fellow struck up a conversation and asked if I'd like to have a cup of coffee with him. A cup of *coffee!* In the *afternoon?* I thought—how queer!—and turned him down on the spot. Instead, I brought home people like Jack Doheny (his father owned a liquor store, no doubt the real attraction), who carried a pint of Jim Beam in his sock and spent about half of every year in the Deer Island jail for petty theft and DUIs. Or Mario, the musclebound longshoreman from East Boston who took the key from my purse while I was passed out, came back the next night when I was working, and ripped off the brand-new eight-hundred-dollar stereo Terry had lent me. A normal person would have called the cops. How manly, I thought, and instantly developed a giant crush on the guy. I called his apartment, stalked him at Misty's—"You have my key, don't be a stranger!"—and made such a general nuisance of myself it's a wonder he didn't come over and rip off the rest of my meager possessions just to shut me up.

Just as I had a longing for human connection, I seemed to have an equally strong urge that was hell-bent on keeping it

forever beyond my reach. I couldn't see that true human connection requires the willingness to be present and feel vulnerable and grow. I couldn't see that because drinking was a fake
way to feel better, everything it generated was fake, too: fake
conversations, fake camaraderie, fake sex, all of which only
made me feel more desperately alone than ever. It was mortifying to realize that other people, usually ones to whom I considered myself vastly superior, saw my dilemma, too. "You're
smaht, Heathah," Pinhead observed one night from behind
the bar, rolling a toothpick in his mouth, "but you don't have
any common sense." What a cretin, I thought, and ordered
another double gimlet.

I once heard a sober alcoholic say that drinking never
made him happy, but it made him feel like he was *going* to be
happy in about fifteen minutes. That was exactly it, and I
couldn't understand why the happiness never came, couldn't
see the flaw in my thinking, couldn't see that alcohol kept me
trapped in a world of illusion, procrastination, paralysis. I
lived always in the future, never in the present. Next time,
next time! Next time I drank it would be different, next time
it would make me feel good again. And all my efforts were
doomed, because already drinking hadn't made me feel good
in years.

twenty

Here we do not have a lasting city;
we seek a home that is yet to come.

—Hebrews 13:14

I still went up to New Hampshire for Mother's Day, Father's Day, all the major holidays, and my birthday. Skip had moved to California, Jeanne was working as a nurse to support her teenage son, Joe was in Hawaii surfing. The rest of my siblings were still around and, along with my parents, formed my usual captive audience as we sat around the dining-room table eating, telling jokes, and, in my case, rather heavily drinking. "Hey, Dad, is there any more Bud?" I'd ask, tripping out to the breezeway where there always seemed to be a six-pack or two on ice. On really special occasions, he'd lay in a few bottles of Lancer's or Mateus, and as the night progressed, there was always the gallon of Popov vodka in the cabinet next to the sink.

But back in Boston, Terry was my main emotional support, and in spite of our work schedules and constant hangovers, we continued to explore the city. Some places you
could bring yourself to visit *only* when hungover: Revere
Beach, for example. Revere was the apotheosis of tacky Italian culture, and a trip there couldn't have differed more
sharply from the fond ocean-bound memories of my childhood. Instead of riding my bicycle down tree-lined Atlantic
Avenue, Terry and I took the Blue Line, hurtling through an
underground tunnel with clots of sullen subway travelers. Instead of a paper bag with a tuna sandwich in it, I clutched a
large cardboard cup of coffee or, if in the midst of a major
bender, beer. Instead of pedaling past Runnymede Farm, my
heart quickening as the glinting water came into view, the car
screeched to a halt and spewed us out at Wonderland (a dog-
racing track) station.

Here we emerged into blinding light; picked our way
across a giant parking lot of heat-radiating asphalt; and, as-
saulted by the mingled smells of Coppertone, onion rings,
and car exhaust, hit the strip. This, too, bore no resemblance
to the beach of my youth, where varicose-veined mothers
draped sweatshirts over their thighs so as not to burn, stoop-
shouldered fathers cowered in the shade of L.L. Bean um-
brellas, and albino-pale children squinted over their plastic
sand pails. Revere looked like a combination staging ground
for the Mister and Miss World bodybuilding contests and an
advanced melanoma ward. As far as the eye could see were
bulked-up bodies burned black by the sun and smeared with

what appeared to be Crisco. It was like a convocation of Peking ducks, if Peking ducks smoked.

New Hampshirites often communed with nature at the beach, quietly combing the shoreline for periwinkles or splashing themselves with healthful salt water, but the people at Revere parked their Caddies, blasted classic rock from the radio, and set up lawn chairs on the broiling-hot sidewalk, reaching into humongous coolers for beer, subs, and chips. Babes in bikinis and rhinestoned mules held foil reflectors to prematurely wrinkled faces, while beside them, their boyfriends scratched their scorched, toned abs with the kind of narcissistically vacant stare that says, "Can I help that I'm a fuckin' stud?" "Four o'clock, check it out," Terry would say out of the corner of his mouth, and I'd look over to see a guy with twenty pounds of gold around his neck, a hairy, greased-up stomach, and a minuscule pair of Speedo bathing trunks clinging obscenely to every bulge and cranny of his genitals, sprawled out on a chaise longue like a beached whale. Age meant nothing to these people, and seventy-year-olds paraded around as proudly as teenagers, hacking like coal miners from their Benson and Hedges: the shriveled dugs of the betel-nut-colored women sagging forlornly in the cups of their two-pieces, the chest hair of the wizened, mahogany-skinned men gone white. Don't get me wrong, I liked a good tan as much as the next person, but I had nowhere near the discipline and stamina of these folks.

After picking our way through the crowded sand, we'd find a place to spread out our towels and Terry would unload "our" duffel bag (he always carried it), which was stocked with packs of Winstons, tubes of Bain de Soleil, and our books. We'd lie there: complaining about our jobs, examining each other's armpits, feet, teeth, and hair, playing the million-dollar game: "For a million dollars would you go on prime-time TV and have sex with Henry Kissinger?" "No, but for seven hundred and fifty thousand I might lick his feet." . . . "For a million dollars would you go on prime-time TV and have sex with Paul Lynde?" "For a million dollars I'd have sex with Paul Lynde, Wally Cox, *and* Rose Marie." . . . Then Terry would run across the street for Diet Cokes and salted cashews, and we'd smoke and kick off greenheads and flip through magazines till it was time to go to Kelly's Roast Beef.

Kelly's was a Revere Beach institution, and it had a routine all its own. First we'd stand in line for ten or fifteen minutes, making fun of people's Bawstan accents and craning our necks to get a look at the possibly cute short-order cooks as we approached the window, then we'd put in our order for fried clams, or cheeseburgers and French fries, then we'd wait some more to pick it up, get extra packets of ketchup and tartar sauce, tote everything back to our towels in a gray cardboard box, scarf it all down in about two minutes, and say, "Oh gross, I feel so fat."

We'd try to lie back down for a while, but by that time we'd be sunburned and restless, so we'd go to some divey bar across the way—the Hi-d-Ho, the Silver Dollar—have a few watered-down drinks while watching *The Price Is Right* on the overhead TV, and weave back to the subway and home. Like I said, some things you could do *only* when hungover.

* * *

Actually I was hungover almost all the time, and since Terrence—basically the only other human being I could stand—was spending more and more time with Stephen, I was spending more and more time by myself. Stephen was a painter—he did Jean-Michel Folon–like pastels; say, a row of men holding kites in one hand and their heads in the other—who was generous, tolerant, good-humored; drank, if at all, moderately; and didn't have a neurotic bone in his body. Plus he was rich. And good-looking. And gay. All of which made me feel ever-so-slightly disadvantaged and wounded—and my way of dealing with wounds had always been to crawl into my cave and isolate.

Maybe that was why, when you got right down to it, it wasn't the Arboretum, or Symphony Hall, or the Isabella Stewart Gardner Museum I liked best about Boston. It was the weird places, the desolate places, the places peopled by misfits, loners, losers. There were a slew of them: the Hillbilly Ranch, a white-trash country-western bar down by the Greyhound station on Park Street; the English Tea Room in the Back Bay, where a mummified waitress parked a giant silver bowl of salad drenched with oversweetened dressing on your table before you'd even opened the menu.

But perhaps my favorite hangout was the Beacon, a restaurant located on the ground floor of the Emerson Hotel for Men, "men" being a euphemism for down-and-out, wet-brain drunks. The food was a step below hospital fare, and the cafeteria-style line was run by Fran, a cross between a seventy-five-year-old, eighty-pound woman and a methamphetamine-addicted parakeet. "What daya want?" she'd squawk. "Move along if ya can't make up your mind, I don't have all day." So I'd order an English muffin grilled in lard and a cup of sludge-like coffee and, along with the other rheumy-eyed, tubercular-coughing, diabetic-ulcerated-footed patrons, move along to a table with an overflowing ashtray, a torn-up Megabucks ticket, and half a fried egg strewn across it.

Ironically, in view of its name, the Beacon was located on a sunless side street and illuminated by twenty-watts maximum bulbs that kept the place bathed in a kind of perpetual dusk. With my fellow dregs of humanity—penny-ante drug dealers, low-level pimps—shuffling through the gloom, I felt right at home. You could get a Miller after eleven a.m., and I spent so much time up there writing in my journal, smoking Winstons, and trying to kill my hangovers with a little hair of the dog that I committed the numbers of my favorite jukebox songs to memory: Bob Seger's "Main Street"—230; "Luckenbach, Texas"—117.

Every once in a while, I'd sober up for a few days, decide to improve my image, and make my way through the cobblestoned streets, across the Common, and down Summer Street to Filene's Basement, a place so near and dear to the hearts of Bostonians that the waitresses at Lombardo's called it simply "the B." The B was part Moroccan bazaar, part yard sale: chockablock with bins of bras, tables of tops, rolling racks of dresses, pants, coats. Jewelry, lingerie, handbags, shoes: the B had it all. Not just any clothes, but one-of-a-kind, up-upscale clothes for ridiculously low prices. You had to wade through a lot of dross, but you could find suede jackets, crocodile belts, linen shirts with hand-rolled seams and covered buttons that were sold in the kind of expensive Newbury Street boutiques I myself felt too lowly to even enter, much less shop at.

Markdowns were taken every seven, fourteen, and twenty-one days, and after that the stuff was practically free. Clothes would be flying through the air like confetti, and women would be making their way to the nearest mirror laden down like camels (things went so fast you nabbed first and sorted out later), and people of all ages, sizes, and body types and both sexes would be standing in the aisles stripped down to their underwear (there were no dressing rooms), tugging clothes on and off as fast as they could, and slapping away the hands of would-be snatchers. Cries of "Quitcher grabbin'!" and "Hey, that's mine!" rang out, and the cashiers couldn't ring up the purchases fast enough. I still have a Giorgio Armani coat I bought down there in the late seventies, a beautiful slate-gray/olive-green wool, with little pleats on either side and nice deep pockets, marked down from $1500 to $175.

Later, I would get far, far beyond the point of caring about, or being able to afford, clothes, and would go around for months in the same ripped jeans and raggedy sweater. But in those days, the B was still a place of light and warmth. In those days, I still thought things might change.

The other place I went to by myself all the time was the movies. In those pre-VCR days, movies—especially old movies—were a very big deal. I mostly went to matinees, partly because they were cheaper, partly because I usually worked at night, and partly because, again, I liked being with my own kind—the socially marginalized, the ones with service or no jobs: I liked being with people as long as I didn't have to talk to them. Paul's Mall, a little below-street-level place on upper Boylston Street, had double-feature matinees for a buck twenty-five, and my other haunt was the Brattle in Harvard Square. The Brattle was a repertory house that dated back to beatnik days—guys in berets were still drinking watered-down mint mochas at the nearby Café Algiers—and it was almost always playing something you could sink your teeth into. I went to the Humphrey Bogart retrospective, the John Ford and John Huston and Sir Laurence Olivier retrospectives, the Peter Lorre retrospective, the Gloria Grahame retrospective. I saw Buñuel's *Los Olvidados* and Max Ophüls's *The Earrings of Madame De . . .* and Fassbinder's *The Bitter Tears of Petra von Kant*. I sat on one of the worn red velveteen seats in the drafty balcony and watched *Casablanca*, and when the lights went up I sat there some more, stunned that I had walked the earth for twenty-six years ignorant of such magic.

I was hungry for stories—anyone's story but my own: gazing raptly up at the screen, I might almost have been praying. I'd smuggle in a Black Forest ham and Havarti sandwich from Formaggio and a French roast from the Coffee Connection and, safe in the dark for a few hours, forget who and where I was. Those were good times, and, even now, I'm sorry they had to end.

twenty-one

O how could we sing
the song of the Lord
on alien soil?

—Psalm 137

Albert was a generous friend and a loyal roommate, but I missed my solitude, and when he brought a yipping shih tzu named Lloyd on board, I knew it was time to go. That's the kind way to put it, anyway. I'd begun keeping a journal, and one entry from that time begins: "I was looking forward to a few days of solitude, notwithstanding that hideous pooch whose hard little black shits are beginning to sprout like poisonous mushrooms all over the apartment," and goes on to apply such phrases as "fetid miasmic air," "clammy atmosphere of a sickroom," and "yellowing newspapers, stiff with dried urine and smeared with feces" to describe poor Albert's bedroom.

I soon found a new apartment, an overpriced studio

around the corner and down a block on Phillips Street. This place had a very strange floor plan, the "living room" being no wider than a corridor, with a windowless bath half a level up to the right and, to the left, a kitchen nobody taller than four and a half feet could stand up straight in. Still, it was a pleasant change to be on my own, and for a few months all went well. I painted the bedroom, bought flowers at Haymarket, and even held a couple of dinner parties. Things took a turn for the worse, however, the night I came home from Misty's, threw a rotting wad of hamburger on to cook, and promptly passed out. I woke to the wail of a fire alarm, smoke billowing through the neighbor-filled hall, and the apartment swarming with men in yellow raincoats, one of whom was angrily brandishing a frying pan containing what appeared to be a charcoalized hockey puck.

"Honey?" Terry said gently when I relayed the story. "Stephen's going back to Nashville for a couple of months, and, well, maybe you and I need to take a little break from Boston, too."

And so, inspired by a pastiche of images drawn from the works of Somerset Maugham, Colette, and Jean Rhys, we secured passports, packed approximately fifty times too many clothes, and jetted off to Europe. Our first stop was Paris, where our main goal was to find a bar that served absinthe. Like the dazed-looking couple in the Degas painting, we, too, aspired to slouch over a café table nursing glasses of a sickly green liquid, and the fact that Baudelaire had reputedly been driven insane by the substance only sharpened our resolve to locate our own supply. Unfortunately, we soon found it had been declared illegal, making it necessary to experience the City of Light, in my case at least, through a haze of rotgut *vin rouge* instead.

Much of this took place in room 5 of the Hôtel de la Loire, which was located on the Left Bank at 20 Rue du Sommerard, across the street from a little shop that sold cheese and wine and was always maddeningly closed during those prime afternoon hours when you were coming out of the worst of your hangover and desperately needed a drink. This was often the time of the day in which I'd be moved to write in my journal: "Once again in the throes of a tempestuous biting hangover brought on by too much red wine. My nerves are on edge to say the very least . . ." "I swear to God my clothes have never been so dirty in all my born days. It has gotten to the point where I cannot bear to put my feet on the floor and face that ravaged heap of filth one more time. Terrence is perfectly content wallowing in his own ordure, of course." "It's been two days now since we've been drunk. The strain is visible; we are surly and uncommunicative. By one o'clock we were on the threshold of the DT's and purposefully raced from supermarket to kiosk to tobacco store to patisserie for booze, smokes, newspaper and food . . ."

Room 5 was fin de siècle and freezing cold, with high ceilings, wrought-iron shutters, drafty windows, and a double bed that sagged in the middle to form a trough that was always filled with the sharp little crumbs from baguettes. Here, Terry and I ate, smoked, read, slept, and amused ourselves by blasting each other with fumes from our ethanol-laced breath.

Whoever woke up first in the morning would light a cigarette, position their face two inches above the other person's and, in their chummiest voice, say, "H-h-h-h-h-h-hiiiiiiii!" At which point the sleeping person would open his or her eyes and yell, "That's disgusting! Get away from me, you animal!" (our way of saying I love you), thus kicking off yet another day of "fun."

In spite of our otherwise slothful ways, we were dutiful, innocents-abroad tourists, and way too imbued with the Protestant work ethic to stay in bed for long. We'd haul ourselves up, get dressed, and—while Terry did his trick of pursing his lips together till they turned white and pretending he was a duck, and I employed my execrable French—head for the nearest café to swill *cafés au lait*, eat *croissants au chocolat*, and plan the day's itinerary. Being unversed in the ways of travel I had brought along a completely impractical wardrobe of wrinkle-prone silk shirts, thin linen jackets that were no help at all in a Paris winter, and totteringly high-heeled suede shoes. The chic French women, nibbling at their brioche, looked through me as if I were invisible, and the debonair French men, downing their morning shots of marc, looked mainly at Terrence. "I hate the French," I wrote in my journal. "They're all so mean!"

Clutching our *Lonely Planet* guide and Metro maps, we visited the Louvre, the Beaubourg, the Tuileries, and, my personal favorite, *les égouts*—the underground sewers. We made pilgrimages to the Dôme, the Select, and the Closerie des Lilas, the bars Hemingway and Fitzgerald had frequented. We thumbed through books at Sylvia Beach's Shakespeare &

Company, and took each other's pictures at the Place de l'Opéra and, from the top of the Eiffel Tower, surveyed all twenty *arrondissements*.

We ate *ficelles* from the *boulangerie* and *oeufs en gelée* from the *charcuterie* and *éclairs* from the *patisserie*, and it was all very bright and gay, and the whole time I was completely paranoid and depressed. I think it was in Paris I realized that there was something very different about the way I drank and the way Terry drank. At the time, he, too, drank like a fish, but his drinking wasn't a slavering compulsion like mine was. He might have still been trying to find his way in the world, but he wasn't wracked with guilt, shame, and self-loathing the way I was. He wanted a boyfriend, just like I did, but he wasn't engaging in the same depraved, self-destructive behavior I was.

I was closer to Terry than anyone on earth, and the knowledge that there was a chasm between us that I couldn't explain or articulate filled me with a whole new kind of loneliness. I didn't know that I was partly lonely for my own self ("I attempt to figure out who or what is the real me—the one who reads myself to sleep and commits poetry to memory, or the one who sits at the bar in a drunken stupor . . ."). I didn't know that I was lonely to write. I didn't know that the beauty of Paris—l'Arc de Triomphe, the flying buttresses of Notre Dame, the Pont Neuf with snow falling on it—only made me feel lonelier than ever because the human and divine love behind that beauty seemed to exist, along with, increasingly, the whole rest of the world, in a different realm than the one I inhabited. I sensed without being able to articulate it that my malady was spiritual, and when in a bookstore I came by chance across *The Confessions* and St. Augustine's famous "Our souls are restless till they find themselves in Thee," I thought, I'm sure that's true—for other people.

One night we became "foully inebriated" (my favorite phrase at the time) in our room and insisted on rounding the soirée off with a jaunt to a neighborhood café. There we sat in our disheveled state, red-rimmed eyes swollen, making semi-intelligible conversation about our fellow patrons: the buck-toothed hag who appeared to be a prostitute, the old lech in the threadbare cravat. Having lived on bread, cheese, and apricot jam for the last three weeks, as usual we were starving.

"Wouldn't it be nice to have one of Nanny's roast chickens right now?" Terrence mused. "I can just smell it coming out of the oven, all nice and brown . . ."

"Don't even start," I snarled.

"Mashed potatoes, maybe some homemade rolls . . ."

"Shut *up!*"

"Stuffing, gravy, butter . . ."

And because I was confused and homesick and hungry, I picked up my glass of red wine and threw it in Terry's face.

"Honey!" he said, groping for a napkin. "That stuff costs three francs a glass!"

"Oh Terry I'm so sorry," I said, dabbing at the stains in his shirt. "I don't know what got into me . . ."

We laughed it off the next morning, but it said more than even I'd known about my disordered psyche and it shocked me. I'd shown hostility, in the lowest-possible-class kind of way, to Terrence—my friend, my protector, someone who had never showed the slightest hostility to me and, to this day, it is one of the moments I most wish I could undo.

We went on to England (weak draft beer), Florence (Campari), and Madrid (sickeningly sweet sangria), but, again as reflected in my oh-so-sunny journal, my mood never lifted. Of an organ recital at the basilica of St. Francis of Assisi: "We were forced to sit around for half an hour listening to the incomprehensible droning of a Spanish priest . . ." Of the toddlers gamboling among the cypresses in the Boboli Gardens: "I become more firmly convinced each day that I will never bear a child. They are ODIOUS." Of a train ride on the vaunted Orient Express: "A couple, of indeterminate racial origin, entered our compartment and immediately began necking. This was repulsive, but not beyond my stamina. Next appeared on the scene a portly Italian, red of face, greasy hair, cheap cologne, pudgy fingers. Seating himself across from me, he began unabashedly to fondle his genitalia . . ."

Traveling made me realize I liked the thought of travel, reading about travel, the anticipation of travel, and I hated traveling itself. It was all too much: the awkwardness and inconvenience of a foreign language, the welter of sounds and sights, the obligation to keep one's interest up. My idea about art was not to look at a hundred paintings, but to look at one for half an hour, then go back to the hotel, stare at the wall while biting my fingernails, and think about it. I'd get overstimulated and tired and then I'd realize I wasn't worthy of traveling, I was a dullard, I didn't know anything about anything, I had attention deficit disorder, people were grotesque, and all I wanted to do was eat. Every so often something would pique my interest—a carnivorous beetle with rat-sized claws in the British Natural History Museum, a glacéed pineapple in the window of Au Bon Marché—and I'd perk up momentarily, only, within minutes, to sink back into my torpor.

Then we visited Morocco. Morocco, I soon discovered, is no place for a paranoid. It was a country that seemed to operate entirely without the benefit of soap, water, or toilet paper; all trains appeared to have been designed to transport livestock, not people; buzzing black flies covered all food. Men pointed and hissed; eight-year-olds sold themselves for cigarettes; thieves and mutants thronged the squares. Also I was stoned on insanely strong hash the whole time and there was *no booze* except, I never figured out why, in the city of Meknes.

Greece seemed a good idea at that point, and on the island of Syros, drinking retsina at the High Life Café, I picked up a soldier named Nicholas, a sinister hey-hey-hey character who looked like a cross between Sammy Davis, Jr., and Jethro from *The Beverly Hillbillies* and, it transpired in his room later that night, wanted me to put out cigarettes on the back of his hand.

"He was a total creep," Terrence summed up when we got back to Paris, which was all the encouragement I needed. I bade Terry farewell—we were supposed to fly home the next day—hopped on the Orient Express, and was back in the High Life within thirty-six hours. I did see Nicholas again, but the main attraction this time around was a merchant marine shipful of British sailors on which I missed by a hair stowing away to Peru.

Broke, I had to wire my parents for the plane fare home. Flying over the Atlantic swilling Dewar's, I wrote in my journal, "How have I changed? What have I learned? That I hate cheap wine and people suck the world over."

Terry met me at Logan with a bottle of Mouton Cadet. "Welcome home, my love!" he cried. "We'll always have Paris!"

twenty-two

Grant me sweet Christ the grace to find—
Son of the living God!—
A small hut in a lonesome spot
To make it my abode.
                    —St. Manchan of Offaly,
                        a convert of St. Patrick's

Back in Boston, I swallowed my pride, asked for my loathsome job back at Cherrystones, and resumed my life at Misty's with a vengeance. Stephen had moved back to Nashville for good while we were gone, initiating a long-distance romance with Terry and bequeathing him sole custody of his loft. Perhaps it was no surprise I was having a teeny problem with my own rent, and when I got served with an eviction notice right before Christmas, Terry heaved a silent sigh and said, "Come on over and stay with me till you find another place," which we both knew would be when hell froze over. So that very weekend I threw my paltry belongings into plastic garbage bags, Tommy came down with his pickup to haul the furniture, and I moved my headquarters across Cambridge and down Stanford to Merrimac Street.

121 Merrimac was the home I'd been looking for all my life, a six-story wedge-shaped brick building that looked like a cross between a condemned sweatshop and a skid-row mission. The front door, a massive slab of battered battleship-gray steel, opened to the smell of unwashed hair, a bare concrete floor, and the kind of grimly institutional stairwell used to connect jail tiers. On the landings (the elevator had been broken for decades), slamming doors echoed, underfed dogs roamed, and haunted, sickly looking men lurked in shadowy corners.

One of the city's last remaining SROs (single-room occupancies), the building was mostly divided into tiny Sheetrocked warrens that people rented out by the night or the week. For $250 a month, utilities included, we ourselves had a spacious triangular loft on the fifth floor, with shopworn hardwood floors, brick walls, and a ceiling of stamped tin. Two tall arched windows gave onto a view, albeit obstructed, of the western skyline; there was plenty of room, so we could both spread out—Terry's bed was beside the makeshift bookcase, near the middle of the room, and mine was at the other end, by the desk; and, for once during a New England winter, I couldn't complain about the cold. Antique radiators shot clouds of steam that melted the ice on the panes, condensed on the overhead pipes, and dripped thick brown water on the pole where we hung our clothes: it was like a polluted sauna in there. I settled right in, lounging around in my underwear drinking Terry's gin, playing Terry's Tammy Wynette albums at full blast, and writing in my journal about how depressed and lonely I was with one of Stephen's left-behind Mont Blanc pens.

Merrimac Street, I soon found, had its own delightful set of mores. There was no kitchen; we cooked on a hot plate. There was no buzzer; when someone came to visit, we put the key in a duffel bag and lowered it down to the sidewalk by rope. An S&M gay bar blasted disco till two in the morning from the ground floor; Chet's Last Call, a punk-rock club, bordered the back alley; and across the street stood the Lindemann Mental Health Center, a block-square psych hospital that provided Merrimac Street with such a steady stream of residents that Terry and I were convinced the landlord had a deal worked out with the guy at the discharge desk.

Our neighbors—drunks, drug addicts, paranoid schizophrenics—were a colorful lot who hung out on the front stoop drinking paper-bag-wrapped beers while waiting for the mailman to bring their welfare checks. One fellow with a filthy yellow beard—Ivan—suffered from Tourette's, and returned even the friendliest greeting with a stream of foul-mouthed invective. Another, whose name I never learned, seemed permanently wound around the third-floor banister, trembling with secret fears, trying to work up the courage to descend (or ascend, I never figured out which).

The building was managed by an Italian fellow named Paulie. Paulie was short, with a matinee-idol profile and luxurious head of silver hair, and would have been handsome except for a set of blatantly false, banana-yellow teeth. "You have *got* to see his 'office,'" Terrence said on the first of the month, dragging me down to a room on the second floor. Every available surface was piled high with ancient newspapers and corroding books. In one corner, almost buried beneath an avalanche of crumbling *National Geographics*, was a piano; in another, a doorless refrigerator. Strips of flypaper, black with insects, dangled from the ceiling; old *Playboy* calendars curled from the walls; and the grime-caked windows emitted so little light you could have set up a projector in the middle of a summer's day and shown porno movies. Paulie was sitting at an old rolltop desk, eating a meatball sub. As Terry handed him the rent check, a rat crept from the shadows and began stealing along the baseboard. Something was stuck to its back leg–a tissue? I thought, then got a good look and realized it was a used condom.

After that I couldn't get enough of the place and was constantly inventing excuses–"Did we pay this month already, Paulie? I forgot"–just to go down and check it out. Paulie kept his accounts in a dog-eared ledger stained with coffee and mustard, and he might not have looked that sharp but he knew how much everyone owed down to the penny. The longtime residents saw him as a kind of father figure–why, I don't know, as diplomacy was scarcely Paulie's strong suit–and there was always a crowd of guys milling around waiting to register a complaint, lodge an excuse, or beg forgiveness. "Ya dipshit!" he'd scream. "Wadya mean your check didn't come? Who else would put up with this crap? Ya don't have it tomorrow, you're out on your ass, youse hear me?" The guy would shuffle dejectedly off, but I'd al-

ways see Paulie remonstrating with him in the corner of
some dank landing a few hours later, and nobody ever
seemed to get kicked out.

All this closeness made for a one-big-happily-dysfunc-
tional-family feel, but perhaps the homiest feature of my new
abode was that the entire floor—there were five other units besides ours—shared a single bathroom. It was located at the
end of the hall, and guaranteed every time you needed to use
it, not only was someone already in there, someone else
would be standing outside toting a toothpaste-laden toothbrush, or clutching a towel and a bar of soap, or pounding on
the door yelling, "Hurry the fuck up! Ya been in there for
hoahs!"

Inside, the walls were splotched with blood, the toilet
floated in a sea of dust, and a bare lightbulb, with a pull chain
of frayed string, hung from a single stripped wire. Folks at
Merrimac Street had one major goal—getting high—and they
weren't about to let a little matter like personal hygiene inter-
rupt the flow. Around the edge of the sink was a necklace of
brown stains where cigarettes had burned down while people
brushed their teeth or washed their dishes or shaved, and
outside the shower—a freestanding unit with flimsy metal
walls—someone had thoughtfully set up a wobbly card table
with a top of warped brown veneer. That way when you were
getting ready to go out you could bring in a drink and a cigarette, set them beside your towel, and snake your wet hand
out from behind the mildewed plastic curtain every few seconds for a drag or a sip. That way you didn't have to go
unanesthetized for even five minutes.

* * *

I was living with Terry, but it was starting to dawn on me that in some ways I had more in common with the other residents than with him. Spurred on by guilt, longing, and a rare moment of humility/sanity in which I realized everybody had to start somewhere, I signed up for a writing class at Harvard Extension. My professor encouraged me so strongly that I went so far, with almost unimaginable trepidation, as to submit a piece to the *Christian Science Monitor*.

One piece, to one place—and when it was rejected, I broke down, mourned for months, and, coming out of it, squared my shoulders against all future hurt. Well, that's over, I told myself. I'm not a writer after all.

twenty-three

And they knew Him in the breaking of
bread . . .

—Luke 24:30–31

One—possibly the only—perk of the restaurant business
was that on my days off I could go to the places where
my friends worked and eat and drink for practically free.
Terry's pal Kevin tended bar at the Rat in Kenmore Square,
and after sitting there swilling Johnnie Walker Black and eating buffalo wings all afternoon, we'd get a bill for, oh, say,
$7.98. (Of course it never ended up being that much of a bar-
gain, because then we'd leave about a fifty dollar tip). Dot's
shift at Misty's began Saturday morning at eleven, and you
can be sure I was there at ten-thirty sharp, "helping" her
count her bank and sipping gratis Stoli. Then there were the
nights when Terry and Albert invited me to Lombardo's.
"Here's that martini you wanted," Terr would say, setting

down a double before I'd even taken off my coat. "I believe you wanted a salad?" Albert would simper, casually dropping off a fake parquet bowl, and beneath a few innocent-looking leaves of iceberg lettuce I'd find six cocktail shrimp, ten anchovies—which I loved—and half a pound of provolone cheese. Special orders of melon with prosciutto conjured themselves out of thin air; carafes of wine were topped off every time I took a sip; wedges of spumoni, tenderly unwrapped from their waxed paper nests and drenched in claret sauce, appeared on my table as if by magic, and when I asked for the bill they'd say, "Oh forget it, they've been tipping good tonight."

Eventually I got to know the people Terry and Albert worked with almost as well as they did. Rudy, the maître d', wore a baby-blue ruffled shirt and a tuxedo jacket and, imperious finger held aloft above his movie-star hair and tanning-salon-bronzed face, managed to ferry hundreds of people to their tables each night without moving his neck: Terrence did a perfect imitation of him, swathing regally through an imaginary crowd and murmuring, "Two, please. Follow back." Angelo was the resident bookie; Erminilda sold hot Joan & David shoes out of the ladies' room; and Jimmy D., a waiter with a cast in one eye, got us into the Caffè dello Sport for after-hours cappuccinos with *sambuca*, a coffee bean nestled in the bottom of each shot glass.

But the one who really took a shine to Terry was Bella, the part-time receptionist. Bella had tragically dark eyes, platinum-blond hair swept back in a shoulder-length flip, and the plush curves of a born cook. She was always bringing in twenty-pound lasagnas or sheet pans of tiramisu for the wait-staff, and one night when we were hanging out having after-work drinks she said, "Come over Sunday, Tay-uh, you and Heathah. I'm cooking."

Bella lived in a nondescript brick building, but from the luscious smells wafting down the hallway that afternoon, I knew we'd entered some kind of eighth culinary wonder of the world. When we walked into the kitchen—linoleum, doilies, crucifixes—the table was already covered with huge platters of food. There were antipasto platters with three kinds of salami, marinated red peppers, olives, celery. There were casseroles of veal cutlets, ziti baked with cheese, rapini sauteed in garlic and hot pepper. There were fried calamari with lemon, tortellini stuffed with ricotta and parsley, and three more pots bubbling on the stove. "I've got an *aglio olio* going," Bella explained, "and some shrimp and scallops, and that's gravy in the back." I peered in, expecting to see the brown stuff you put on turkey, but gravy to Bella was spaghetti sauce, and hers was so loaded with sausage, chicken, and pork chops that you could have stood a spoon up in it.

Pointing to a gargantuan plate, she said, "Here, try some potatoes and eggs," which doesn't sound like much but was a revelation, a cloud of textures and tastes that could only have been made by someone with the kind of sublime culinary in-tuition that knew the exact size to mince a clove of garlic, the temperature butter should be to scramble eggs in, the number of turns to take with a pepper grinder.

A parade of shirtless, impossibly handsome teenage boys— Bella's sons and their friends, I soon gathered—began passing through: sitting down, ingesting huge quantities of food and leaving with nary a comment beyond "No eggplant, Ma?" or "Where's the gnocchi?" I was stupefied at their failure to fall to their knees and give thanks, but throughout the course of the afternoon learned this was because Bella more or less cooked this way all the time. "Last Sunday I made the linguine from scratch," she apologized, throwing a pound of De Cecco on to boil, "but my Auntie Cristina was in the hospital this week."

There was never a point where Bella sat down and said, "Okay, dinner's ready"; it was one continuously replenishing, never-ending feast. She nibbled a little, and cooked, and chatted, and sat down, and got up and cooked some more, all with such easy humor and unselfconscious grace if I'd felt any more at home I would have gone into the living room and eaten from a reclining position on the couch. This was cooking on a level I hadn't known existed, cooking that couldn't be taught or learned, cooking that came from some deep wellspring of knowledge that the only reason for having been given any kind of talent is to share it. She was like an artist with an easel, painting a big beautiful picture of hospitality and generosity and nurturing abundance.

After we had eaten to the bursting point, she made espresso in a little silver pot, and brought out cannoli and a cake soaked in rum and two bottles of anisette. We sat for hours, telling stories and jokes, the taste of browned veal and meltingly soft chicken and tomatoes wreathed in basil lingering in our mouths, our hearts warm with hope and love.

Out of some subconscious, innate respect, for once I stayed sober enough to remember the whole night. All in all, it may have been the most glorious meal I ever had.

It seemed very unfair, but what with all this eating and drinking I had put on a few extra pounds. I signed up for an aerobics class at a nearby Glo Stevens, but after the first session—held in a mirrored, carpeted basement on lower Cambridge Street—I saw it would be far too depressing, taxing, and slow to lose weight through the normal route of exercise and cutting calories. With my usual eagerness to do things the hard, genuine way, I determined instead to find a diet doctor. The waitresses at Lombardo's swore by some senile ob-gyn from E.B. (East Boston), so one Friday afternoon I gave him a call. The phone rang eight times and then a man who sounded like he'd been sleeping all day and did not identify himself as a doctor answered. Perfect, I thought, and made an appointment for the next week.

Naturally the guy was a complete quack. He worked out of his house, and anyone who has ever gone real-estate hunting will recognize the feeling I experienced when I walked down his street the following week, located his address, and discovered that his was the shabbiest, most rundown dwelling on the block. In the living room, a few faded medical journals were strewn across a dusty coffee table, a bubblegum machine stood next to a pair of ancient scales, and tacked to the wall was an ancient chart of the female reproductive system (you just knew he did abortions, too). Sitting on the stained beige sectional, their limbs jerking like marionettes, were

three other women, all of whom appeared to be in the final
stages of anorexia. I was maybe ten or fifteen pounds overweight myself, but next to them I looked like Marie Dressler.

Sure enough, however, one by one each of them disappeared into the adjacent room and emerged a few minutes
later—sunken eyes aglitter, cadaverous fingers twitching—
clutching a bottle of small yellow pills. When my turn came,
an elderly fellow doddered to the door and, with a liver-
spotted hand, waved me into what transpired to be the
kitchen. The sink was piled high with dishes, the floor was
tacky with grease, and under the table lay an overflowing cat
box. I'd worn my tightest pants so as to appear as fat as possible, and concocted a story about the morbid obesity that
ran in my family, but I needn't have bothered. Barely glanc-
ing at the scale—80, 280, whatever—the "doctor" shuffled over
to the counter, reached into one of those plastic buckets people store kibble in, and counted out ninety of the yellow pills.
"You want to take these in the morning," he quavered. (Duh.)
"One a day."

Naturally I immediately began taking four or five or six a
day. I am an extremely jittery, high-strung person who should
under no circumstances take any kind of stimulant (including
coffee, to which I am helplessly addicted), and this was terrible stuff: coarse, brutal, jarring. To take the edge off, get
through the day without grinding my teeth down to nubs,
and at night fall into even the most tortured, rudimentary
kind of sleep, I had to imbibe more massive quantities of alcohol than ever.

As the weight dropped off like melting snow—and I edged

ever closer to psychosis—it occurred to me that street drugs might be a better bet. I'd done my share of Black Beauties, which were smoother and subtler, but only because some generous fellow waiter or waitress or another had supplied them. I was always glad to swallow someone else's pills or snort someone else's coke, but I'd never cared enough about drugs to buy them on my own. For one thing I was too cheap and for another I was so woefully lacking in street smarts that any dealer worth his or her salt would have immediately ripped me off blind—not to mention that my fine motor skills were so consistently compromised by drinking that I could never have physically maneuvered the hopelessly tricky business of, say, shooting up.

But mostly, I saw pasty-skinned, track-marked drug users as dilettantes, poseurs: to my mind, anyone who still had it together enough to care about the quality of the high, or his or her image, wasn't nearly hard-core enough. For sheer degradation; for throwing one's looks, health, and reputation down the toilet; for a steady diet of rejection, humiliation, loneliness, and anguish; to my mind nothing—especially for a female—trumped being a blackout, falling-down drunk. I was all by myself, out on the knife-edge of self-imposed pain and proud of it. I wasn't good at much else, but the least I could do was suffer.

twenty-four

O Jerusalem, Jerusalem! . . . How often would
I have gathered your children together as a
hen gathers her brood under her wings, and
you would not! Behold, your house is
forsaken . . .

—Luke 13:34–35

One afternoon, lying hungover in bed and miserably
contemplating the prospect of waiting tables that night,
I got the kind of call that made me think maybe there really
was a god. It was Leonard from work informing me that my
fondest wish had come true: Cherrystones had burned to the
ground. Nobody had been hurt, and I was glad to know
they'd managed to save the wine cellar, but the main thing
was that I didn't have to work that night. What were hundreds of thousands of dollars compared to a moment of relief
for *me*?

The relief was short-lived, for a new branch had been due

to open momentarily and the very next week the whole staff was transferred to the new, fancier digs down at the water-front. Where the old restaurant had been neighborly and down-home, now there was valet parking and a receptionist dressed like a model and flowers in the bathroom. Where before we'd had cardboard plates and plastic cups and the specials written slapdash on a blackboard, now there were crystal glasses, real china, a printed menu. Where before it had been about serving plain, fresh fish, now it was about the right preparation, the right wines, making the Boston restaurant scene. We'd never had much contact with the actual owners, but now they were hanging around every night looking down their noses, and making us wear hairnets, and in general acting like they were feudal landowners and we were ignorant slaves. I hated seeing Rose in that environment—it was terrible to witness a genuine, salt-of-the-earth person deferring to such nouveau riche phonies.

I myself proudly scorned any such bowing and scraping, the result being that within weeks I was fired: "Bad attitude," Stanley noted curtly, handing me my last check. Leonard got canned in the same sweep, and commiserating over drinks, we agreed it was a low blow indeed, after all we'd done for them. I felt a momentary pang, realizing the days of unlimited cocktail shrimp had come to a screeching halt, that I'd probably never work with Leonard or Rose again. Still, I told myself, Cherrystones had gotten a little hoity-toity for my taste: maybe it *was* time to move on. So I lowered my sights and landed a job at a place so down-home it actually had the working-man's drink of choice in its name: Spiros's Kebab and Beer.

Spiro's was a little Greek joint in the South End. It had red Naugahyde booths, Formica tables, and an open kitchen, and it was run by the trio of Spiro, Tassos, and Lidia. Lidia and Tassos were married (arranged), and Spiro–the head cook, if you want to call someone who spoons out canned string beans and instant mashed potatoes a cook–was some repulsive kind of relative. I thought I had bad habits when it came to food, but in full view of the customers (most of them being noxious Tufts students, not that they didn't deserve it), Spiro would reach his bare hand into a pan of corn, let the juice drain through his fingers, and stuff a fistful of kernels directly into his mouth. He'd call you over, make you run to the machine and buy him cigarettes, and trail his fat, clammy hand suggestively over yours when you handed him the pack. He had a vicious temper, hurling his spatula to the floor and screaming, "Stupit! Dumbbell!" if you accidentally wrote rare instead of medium rare, or picked up the plate with rice on it instead of French fries. After alternately insulting and grossing out everyone in sight all evening, he'd emerge from the kitchen at closing time, have a few V.O.-and-Cokes and get all expansive and jolly. "Land of opportunity!" he'd beam, raising his glass and brandishing a greasy wad of hundreds. "America! Land of opportunity!" It was enough to make you puke.

Tassos, Spiro's assistant, was bald on top, and had long black hair combed creepily along the sides, and was quiet and

long-suffering, having probably had it drilled into his head
every day since his wedding ten years before that he had married above him. Lidia was stark, ravingly beautiful—perfect
figure, honey-blond hair, green eyes—and cold and spiteful to
the core. She had the soul of Claude Rains's mother in *Notorious*, and to gaze upon her gorgeous face, and hear the cruel,
shrewish words emanating from her mouth, was to experience a jolt of major cognitive dissonance. From her hangout
at the front table, she sized up the customers, made change,
and watched us waitresses like a hawk. If you spent a second
too long in the bathroom, she'd know you were smoking and
come in and yell at you. If you were waiting on a party of
your friends, she'd look over your shoulder to make sure you
were charging for those two rice puddings. No matter how
busy you were running around delivering $3.95 roast chicken
plates and $2.50 slabs of pastitsio (needless to say, the tips
sucked), the minute one of your customers laid their cash
down on a check, you'd hear that piercing, querulous voice
saying, "Regeester! Table six!"

Naturally I considered all this very harsh treatment ("I
despise the people I work for, though I know in part it's my
own fault and at some point I have to 'strive higher'—gross.
Why can't I win Megabucks and devote myself whole-
heartedly to the solitary life of a writer?") and could not have
borne it for a second if not for my co-workers. Joy was tall
and stoop-shouldered, with endearingly snaggled teeth and a
boyfriend who, conveniently for us, tended bar at the dive
next door. Marge, her best friend, had a bushy shag hairdo,
and was short and sturdy and part Greek herself—though,

rolling her eyes in the direction of the kitchen, she begged the rest of us not to hold that against her. The two of them were always inviting me to their "Tuppahweah" and Mary Kay parties, and they were such efficient and matter-of-fact waitresses, and had their heads screwed on so tight when it came to being good workers without kowtowing (a balance I never achieved myself) that it made me feel safe just being around them.

Petra gave the impression of being about three feet tall and four feet wide. She had a thick Russian accent and hacked-off hair dyed a blinding shade of copper red, and was also a terrible table hog, waddling with surprising speed to the front of the restaurant to steer incoming parties to her station. This didn't bother me at all—my goal was always to wait on the least, not the most, possible number of tables—but she also never did any side work. This made it harder on the rest of us—even I at least did my share of side work—but Petra was putting her son through college, so we all cut her some slack.

Then there was Barb. Barb was a tough old babe in her sixties who looked like that Diane Arbus photo of a fierce, big-nosed Puerto Rican woman with thick black painted-on eyebrows and a mole by her nose. "I'm just an old reprobate," she'd say out of the side of her mouth—she was missing a front tooth—and she was such a character that people fought to sit at her tables even though she was the world's worst waitress. Garbling orders; picking up the wrong food; leaving a trail of crumbs, spilled drinks, and broken dishes in her wake; she was like a stately battleship, cutting slowly through the waters of the restaurant with her gigantic bosom. No amount of pressure could induce her to speed up. "Bar-ber-ahhh!" Food get cold! Pick food up *now!*" Spiro would bellow, his face purple with rage. "Yeah, yeah, keep your shirt on," Barb would drawl, and calmly finish the story she was telling to a tableful of captivated customers. Things that made me jumpy and anxious Barb simply tuned out. "Lidia? Ah, phooey on Lidia," Barb would say, waving a man-sized paw. "Don't let her get to you."

Along the right-hand side of the restaurant ran a bar with a TV over it where people came in to drink beer and watch ball games, and where we ordered drinks, paying for them out of our banks. Grant, the head bartender, was married with two sons and taught high school science. Grant was kind of nice, and kind of cute—he looked a little like a blond Clark Kent—except that he was also very slightly psychotic. The night would be going along fine—you'd be joking around and moving smooth and not doing anything that might annoy him, like rushing him while he was waiting on his bar customers, or reciting your drinks in the wrong order—and all of a sudden there'd be dead silence, and you'd look up, and for no apparent reason Grant would be staring at you with a look of pure, burning, homicidal hatred.

The other bartender was Roland, a pudgy mama's boy from the North End who was so good-natured and even-tempered even Lidia liked him. He had this fake, old-Italian-man rant he'd go into when you made a mistake or bugged him for drinks when he was busy. "I'm gonna have-a you put down!" he'd say. "I'm gonna take-a you to Angel Memorial"—Angel Memorial was Boston's big animal hospital—"and

have-a you put down!" Which was funny but, now that I
think of it, sort of sad, too. We were allowed one free post-
work drink, and after fine-tuning the possibilities for months,
with Roland's help I finally settled upon what I was certain,
drop for drop, packed the most potent possible punch: a tum-
bler full of straight Metaxa, a Greek liqueur that tasted exactly like warm paint thinner.

By this point my diet-pill intake had hit an all-time high,
and I eventually got so strung out from lack of sleep and
food—I'd actually come to consider nicotine a *nutrient*—that
my drinking became truly sloppy. One of the things I started
doing at work was ordering cocktails from the bar, pouring
them into coffee cups, and drinking them myself. We all
drank coffee endlessly, and kept our half-drunk cups on a
shelf beneath the far end of the bar, but the danger in putting
one of my drinks there was that one of the other waitresses
might pick it up by mistake—or worse, that Lidia might find it.
One night I got so loaded, and began to feel so untypically
friendly toward my customers, that I bore down on one of
my parties—a pleasant young couple who looked like they
might have been out on their first date—bawled, "Scushe me,
I'm just going to leave thish here a sec," and leaned over to
slosh a ceramic mug brimming with straight Wild Turkey in
between the ketchup bottle and sugar bowl. (Employee of the
Month award, anyone?)

I'm still not entirely sure how it happened—it may have
been a plate of moussaka I brought back because a customer
had complained it wasn't hot enough—but one afternoon I
stopped off for a little too long at Misty's before work and,

when I got in, had words with Spiro. He started it—"Bitch!
Whore!"—but it probably wasn't the smartest personnel move
in the world to call the head cook a pig either, and next thing
I knew he was chasing me down Columbus Avenue with a
rolling pin in one hand and a slotted spoon in the other.
"Land of opportunity!" I called spitefully over my shoulder,
and I felt awful about not getting to say good-bye to the other
girls, but I knew that was going to be the last I ever saw of
Spiro's.

In a way I was glad, but the next morning, lying in bed
with yet another excruciating hangover, I felt scared and appalled on a whole new level. I'd been fired from *Spiro's Kebab
and Beer*. Could a person possibly sink any lower?

twenty-five

Blessed are they whose ways are blameless,
Who walk according to the law of the Lord.
Blessed are they who keep his statutes
and seek him with all their heart.

—Psalm 11

With every drink, the fear of facing who I was, and what I was making of myself, increased. I couldn't imagine continuing, and I couldn't imagine stopping. I lived in constant tension between the longing on the one hand to come alive, create, contribute; and on the other, the obsessive-compulsive drive to self-destruct. I had to do *something*.

And so, as I approached my thirtieth birthday, I did what any sane person would do who was terrified of confrontation, pathologically afraid of public speaking, and so panic-stricken at life in general that she'd become a nightly blackout drinker: I decided to go to law school. One evening I was holding court on my bar stool at Misty's when someone remarked, apropos of my usual obnoxious, loud-mouthed behavior, "You ought to be a lawyer." Bereft of my own ideas, starved for direction, I seized upon this chance comment of a virtual stranger and decided forthwith to build my life around it. Yes, I thought to myself, I *should* be a lawyer! I conveniently set aside the small facts that I had never done any kind of work besides waitressing, that I was incapable of going without a drink for the eight or nine hours a regular job required, that I was not even sure what lawyers did. It was not a very well thought out plan.

Since my hangovers ruled out all possibility of commuting, I focused instead on the fortuitous fact that a law school was handily located mere blocks from both Misty's and my apartment. I applied to just that one place, having sobered up long enough during the LSAT process to secretly hope I'd get turned down and could therefore scrap the whole idea. As luck would have it, however, I got in, at which point, since I'd blabbed the news that I was contemplating doing something besides ruining my liver to everyone I knew—my parents, of course, were thrilled—I felt *obligated* to go.

Oh well, I thought vaguely, maybe law school would change me. Maybe it would make me study so hard I'd *naturally* cut down on my drinking. Maybe it would transform me from a person with a nervous system so sensitive that, when sober, merely being addressed by a fellow human being almost caused me to hyperventilate, into a bold, assertive advocate for victims of racial oppression and gender discrimination. Maybe I would stop feeling disenfranchised and clueless and start being privy to the inner workings of The Law. I had always secretly suspected that everyone but me had been handed a rule book at birth. Now, finally, I would be at the very heart of how things worked.

People sometimes ask me, "How could you have gotten through law school drunk?" My answer is that there is no way I could have gotten through law school if I *hadn't* been drunk. One of the first things on the agenda, for example, was the Moot Court competition, a nerve-racking, nail-biting event that entailed writing a brief on an assigned topic, presenting it to a panel of black-robed alumni, and, as an audience of professors and fellow classmates critiqued your every move, attempting to respond to such hypothetical, unanswerable questions as "How do you propose to reconcile the Rule Against Perpetuities with the equal-protection clause?" or "What is the proximate cause of a counteroffer?" As it turned out, this was a standard first-year law school exercise that the other students, who had actually done some research, and talked to other law school graduates, and informed themselves about what they were going to be doing for the next three years, knew about well in advance. I, on the other hand, was in shock from the moment I heard about it and would certainly not have applied at all had I known it was in store.

We prepared for months: researching esoteric points of law, polishing our papers and listening to endless tips from our fresh-out-of-law-school Legal Skills professor, a woman who dressed in the kind of shapeless blue suits and half bowties worn by female prison guards. She could not impress upon us firmly enough the solemnity of the occasion, the potential effect on our careers, the deference due the corporate lawyers and appeals court judges and Harvard professors who had deigned to grace us lowly students with their presence. The men were to shine their shoes and comb their hair and put on suit coats. We women were not to wear our skirts too short or our heels too high or our earrings too dangly. We were all to dress in conservative colors, speak in a modulated, pleasant voice, and say thank you at the end.

"Now, are there any last questions about how to conduct yourselves from the podium?" she asked. I raised my hand from the back of the room.

"Yes?" she nodded.

"Can we smoke?" I asked.

She didn't even get that it was a joke—hardly anybody did—and that was when I saw that the worst thing about law school was going to be that it lacked all sense of humor.

Time bore me out: as the months passed, I searched in vain for a subject that wasn't deadly boring, dry as dust, and leached of every detail of the kind that makes things interesting in real life. I did work up some affection for a few tort cases if only because, fleshed out, they would have made such great short stories. There was the aunt who sued her five-year-old nephew for battery because when she had gone to sit down in a lawn chair, he had snatched it out from beneath her, causing her to fall and break her hip. There was the woman who sued a stock boy in a grocery store for intentional infliction of emotional distress because she had asked him the price of an item he was marking and he had replied, "If you want to know the price, you'll have to find out the best way you can. *You stink to me.*" There was the jilted lover who had thrown lye in his girlfriend's face, completely disfiguring her. (In an unprecedented show of human interest, the legal textbook writers had thoughtfully added a footnote saying that when the guy had finally gotten out of jail, *she had married him.*)

The one first-year class that really struck a chord, however, was Products Liability. Here, at last, was a universe I recognized: the one where disaster lurked around even the most harmless-looking corner, where trouble troubled you whether you wanted it to or not. One fellow in bed with an arthritic shoulder, Bengay fumes seeping from beneath his pajama top, lit a cigarette and was immolated. Another man decided to help his wife out around the house and was castrated by the vacuum cleaner. A teenage girl at a lunch counter ordered a bottle of Coke and, after partially consuming the contents, discovered it contained a decomposing rat.

The theory of liability in the Coke case was called *res ipsa loquitur*—the thing speaks for itself: there'd so obviously been a screw-up at the bottling plant that the plaintiff was relieved of the usual obligation to prove when the negligence had occurred, exactly what it consisted of, who was responsible. *Res ipsa loquitur*, it came to me as my drinking continued unabated, could be applied to the whole decomposing-rat mess of my life. Something, somewhere along the line, had gone grotesquely wrong. Except with me, there was no one to blame but myself.

* * *

I'd thought law school would help me cut down on my drinking but all it really did, for the first time in my life, was make
me try to control and manage my drinking. As a matter of
fact, the stress of school drove me to try to control everything: weight, drinking, human relationships. "I have ab-
stained from drinking for five days—which is always big
news—and am ergo finding mankind *particularly* loathsome." "I
am now almost preternaturally obese [I probably weighed
130] and have made one of my solemn oaths to lose
weight . . ."

As for my fellow students, I immediately managed to create my usual deprivation-in-the-midst-of-plenty universe: iso-
lating, judging, and compartmentalizing myself right into
avoidance of full intimacy with anyone. At this stage of my
life, I tended to divide straight guys into two completely separate groups—brothers and potential sex partners. Gay guys—
because I *couldn't* sleep with them—I allowed to become soul
mates, gay women I distanced myself from both emotionally
and sexually, and straight women (probably because they
were "my own kind" and I hated myself so much) I tended to
have no use for whatsoever. One Friday evening I dragged
two of my classmates—Wayne, a flamboyant queen, and his
sidekick Beverly—to Misty's. During the course of this rare
night of "socializing" with my peers Wayne not only reiter-
ated the fact of his own gayness, but Bev announced hers as
well. "You didn't know?" she said. "Suffolk is known for its
huge number of bull dykes." I cringed for a moment, thinking
of my own all-denim wardrobe and Converse sneakers, but

then I realized it didn't matter. All the guys were ugly anyway, so who cared?

Back at Merrimac Street, books continued to be my only solace. ("One of my many conceits is that people are basically too boring to endure without the benefit of alcohol, which leads to the bleak Hobson's choice of either staying drunk at a bar or staying home and reading.") And Terrence, for better or worse, continued to be my one guiding light. ("Terry is still and always my saving grace, being quite simply, <u>far and away</u>, my favorite person on the face of the earth. I sincerely believe that, with the possible exception of my parents, he is the only person who <u>appreciates</u> me—or is even capable of doing so.")

He had full access to my journal, and opening it the next morning, I found a note in his handwriting: "11/22/81 Happy Thanksgiving, Heather. I love you with all my heart—and more than anyone else ever will. You are a precious gift from above."

Law school is perfect for an alcoholic because there is only one exam for each course and it is given at the end of the semester. The first year all five courses lasted both semesters. My way of dealing with this was to blithely drink my way through till spring, then to go on the wagon, tear myself away from the abstracted part of my brain where I usually resided, and bury myself in the basement of the library from eight in the morning until ten at night for fourteen consecutive days.

Performance anxiety ratcheted up to its highest possible level, I made insanely detailed outlines, with the exceptions to the exceptions to the exceptions. I underlined case citations in red, and wrote sentences in increasingly microscopic print that snaked around the top, bottom, and side margins, then spilled over to the back of the page. I stapled on addendums and scotch-taped inserts and scribbled cryptic N.B.'s that said, "Only for X-Δ ltd. p'ships" and "Viz. Palsgraf and progeny" and "Cf. ¶ XIII (G) (4) (b)."

Then—eyes gritty from lack of sleep, voice hoarse from disuse ("I am so friggin sick of that library I could take a machine gun to the whole hideous edifice . . .")—I branded all five outlines on my brain, so that I could close my eyes and picture which page any given fact was on, and where on the page, and exactly what it said. In a way, it was my finest hour. Anything that reeks of the hair shirt and the knout, torture, and self-mortification, I'm an expert at, and I'd never studied with such grim intensity in my life.

When the marks came out that summer, I was ranked seventh in a class of 317. I walked around in a daze—awed, elated, proud!—for about ten minutes. And then I panicked, for it came to me that eventually I would have to graduate. I would graduate, people would expect me to get a job, and my fatal flaw would be revealed: that I was completely incapable of extrapolating any of the information I'd memorized so that it might be of practical use. The thought that an actual person might come to me with a problem and expect me to solve it rendered me almost catatonic with fear.

I did not work a single day the whole time I was in law school; by going without new clothing, food, and all entertainment besides a weekly stack of library books, I was able to survive (i.e., buy booze) on student loans and the hundred dollars my loving, oblivious, poverty-stricken parents sent me every other week. I did the drill: Contracts, Evidence, Probate. I learned about *in rem* jurisdiction, hearsay, revocable trusts; I even made it into the inferior of the two law reviews (the Spring '84 issue of the *Suffolk Transnational Law Journal* contains a fascinating commentary on the Longshoremen and Harborworkers' Compensation Act)—but the whole time somehow I knew I wasn't in it the way my classmates were.

While they were networking, I was sitting in my cockroach-ridden loft drinking straight gin out of a Flintstones glass. While they were applying for judicial internships, I was lying in bed, so hungover I was practically hallucinating. While they were discussing the fast track for partner, I was fighting to see any other future for myself than slowly drinking myself to death. One winter morning I rolled into class from a typical night on the town. Chatting with a group of fellow students afterward, I reached into the pocket of my coat and pulled out what I thought were my gloves. The conversation stopped dead. Dangling from my fingers was a pair of my panties.

Maybe the most heartbreaking thing about law school, considering how little I cared about it, was that I really did try. My brief bursts of manic activity might have come in the midst of long bouts of drinking/extreme sloth, but on some level I really did know something was at stake; I really was paying attention. Or maybe it was just my latent competitive streak. People say that drinking indicates a lack of willpower, but whatever the case, it takes almost superhuman strength to maintain the kind of double life I did in law school, and it takes a special kind of strength when not just one life but both lives seem devoid of meaning. I kept thinking of a friend who'd never been able to get the hang of elementary school math: "But what's it *for*?" she'd finally asked her teacher in exasperation. It was only when she'd grown up and discovered math was "for" music, poetry, quantum physics, that she'd caught fire with it. In spite of my initial hopes, however, it was difficult to imagine any such transcendent use of the law.

Law school exam questions were geared toward "issue-spotting," which generated the kind of Rube Goldberg scenario where a drunk in a stolen car picked up a blind hitchhiker, ran a stop sign that had been painted over by pranksters, and collided with a pickup driven by a woman with a weak heart who promptly had a coronary and died. It was easy enough to spot transferred intent and mistake-in-fact and the doctrine that you take the victim as you find him—but what's it for? I wanted to ask after a while. So someone lost on a technicality, and someone else got some money, or someone went to jail, but what was it *for*? Did locking up a murderer help the family of the man he'd killed deal with their grief? Did a big settlement make either party more tolerant or more forgiving? "Why must I be so utterly undisciplined, so moody, dreamy, lazy, despondent, eternally frustrated, unsatisfied and ultimately guilty with the knowledge that it is all MY FAULT?" I wrote in my journal.

My classmates, jockeying for interviews, discussing salaries, seemed unconcerned with such questions. Like the rest of the world, they seemed to have figured out something I didn't know—where they'd come from, where they were going—and moved on.

Perhaps the lowest point of my law school career came the summer before my third year. In his mid-twenties by now, my brother Joe had discovered the joys of drinking on his own. Having forgone college for the moment, he was working construction at the Seabrook Nuclear Power Plant and living in a rented cottage in Portsmouth, and every Friday afternoon I'd take the bus up from Boston, walk through a glass-strewn alley off upper Islington Street, and meet him at the Alibi Room. The Alibi was a complete sleazehole that for some obscure reason—since nobody but a total lush with zero self-esteem would want to join—operated as a private club (a year's membership cost five bucks, two-fifty for a lifetime, the joke went). I'd make my way down a stairway that smelled like a convalescent home, get signed in by a guy with warts all over his face, and there by the duct-taped pool table my beloved brother would be, ordering drinks from a barmaid with a bleach-blond beehive named Vi. Over ninety-five-cent snakebites—vodka and peppermint schnapps—we'd get reacquainted, our conversations taking a John Waters–esque, weirdly incestuous turn: in a touching display of brotherly love, for example, Joe had taken to calling me "Kitten"; while I, having concluded we could no longer bear living in separate states, was contemplating marriage.

After several rounds it would be time to wend our way back to the cottage, throw darts, and trade insults with Joe's friends. Freak had the mushroom pallor that comes from having spent way too much time in a darkened bedroom listening to the Ramones, and The Shadow was a five-foot-two drummer whose perenially unbrushed teeth were the color of moss. We'd eat frozen pizza, drink beer, and, around ten, thoroughly wasted, drive back into town, pile into one of the local clubs, and stagger around the dance floor until last call, or we got shut off, whichever came first.

Joe had a talent for cultivating odd characters, and another of his conquests was Tex, the bald, toothless patriarch of a large family who lived in a trailer behind the cottage. Tex hailed from Abilene, had purportedly traveled north by bus carrying nothing more than the clothes on his back, his battered guitar, and a quart of Four Roses, and was perhaps the biggest liar I have ever met. Though I never quite mastered the rules, the three of us took to playing marathon games of poker. These would start around seven a.m. with a couple of six-packs and Tex strumming "South of the Border," and go downhill from there. By noon, we'd be passing around a bottle of Jack Daniel's, lighting the wrong ends of cigarettes, and nodding off between hands. Tex took full advantage of our soporific state to tell more and more outrageous lies. One afternoon, on the edge of consciousness, I realized that if the story he'd just told were true–ten years as a POW, seventeen as a codebreaker for the FBI, twenty-three touring with Elvis—he would have had to have been something like 110.

"How can that be, Tex?" I slurred. "You haven't lived long enough to fit all that in."

Tex never missed a beat. "*You* go to college," he snapped. "*You* figure it out."

twenty-six

Repairer of the breach, they shall call you,
Restorer of ruined homesteads.

—Isaiah 58:12

E very so often, I'd take the bus up to New Hampshire, but
if things at 108 Post Road weren't quite as bleak as they
were in Boston, the folks there were struggling, too. Joe, having gotten fired from his job at the nuke and temporarily
moved back home, was running up huge phone bills, had
taken to wearing a black T-shirt around the house that read
"Fuck you, I already have enough friends," and was engaged
in a very suspicious wake-sleep cycle that consisted of lying in
bed all day, then staying up till five in the morning reading.
(Joe had extremely eclectic tastes in literature and may be the
only person I have ever met who could, or would want to, simultaneously read the diaries of Samuel Pepys and Jim
Thompson's *The Killer Inside Me*.)

He'd also started a punk-rock band called (what else?) the

Queers and, as a consequence, was attracting a series of alarmingly young girls. The dining room looked the same as ever—laminated Lake Winnipesaukee placemats, Rich's Discount bird feeder outside the window with five sunflower seeds in the bottom of it—and now sharing our meager fare would be, say, a fifteen-year-old with a ring through her nose, lips outlined in black, and lace-up boots of the kind worn by Hitler's SS. "Would you like some more peas, Bambi?" Mom would ask, and Bambi, who it turned out lived up the street and was the daughter of the town librarian, would answer politely, "Why thank you, Mrs. King, I'd love some more peas."

Joe's old high school chum Chad, a sensitive youth with a weakness for folk songs, had also taken up residence—my parents often took in one or another of our stray friends while they were between jobs or apartments—and had gotten a job as a milkman. This required rising at three a.m., which wasn't working out all that well, as he was staying up till two every night getting wasted and listening to songs like "Old Hard-Luck Jim" and "Mary Joined the Union." Three o'clock might have been the middle of the night for most people, but it was just the time when I most craved, and was least likely to find, human company. One morning I went with him on his rounds, standing shotgun in the high-roofed truck sipping Buds and, as the sun rose and the rest of the world prepared to get dressed and put in an honest day's work, spewing cigarette smoke over the bottles of fresh milk and cream and thinking up bastardized lyrics to lovely old campfire tunes like "The Ash Grove."

"Hey, Chadster, how about this?" I slurred, groping in his

pocket for a match. "The ashtray, how graceful, how plainly 'tis speaking, the can-ce-er I'm contracting has language for me . . ."

"Hawr, hawr," he roared. "Grab me a cottage cheese, will ya? Old Lady Leavitt'll have a fit if I don't leave her small curd."

Geordie was the only one at that point who, against all odds, had turned out halfway normal. At twenty-three, he was living in Portsmouth and captaining a commercial fishing boat: the whole family doted on his success. The old man in particular was beside himself with pride, and the rest of us were thrilled because it meant free food. Geordie was always bringing halibut steaks or a bucket of flounder or a couple of three-pound lobsters down to the house—though, as usual, the way it got doled out left us shaking our heads in bewilderment. One night when seven of us were gathered for dinner, Mom brought out a platter bearing a single tiny haddock, albeit nicely blanketed with buttered crumbs, and placed it triumphantly in the center of the table. "Jesus," Geo said out of the side of his mouth. "I thought maybe Mom and Dad would share that one. I didn't think she'd try to feed all of *us* with it."

Little Meddy, a junior in high school by now, had become quiet and withdrawn, unobtrusively making me my grilled cheese sandwiches as usual, then disappearing upstairs. She was holed up in my old room, the walls pink again (Mom had painted over the evidence of my own youthful rebellion): another small depressed brain staring out at the Pit, plotting her escape.

As for Danny, fed up with the bullying that had plagued

him since childhood, he'd taken up, in turn, weightlifting, kickboxing, and karate. He'd switched favorite TV shows from *Lost in Space* to *Kung Fu*. He'd dropped out of high school and started taking bus trips to Boston's Chinatown, returning with vials of Tiger Balm, canisters of ginseng tea, Chow Yun-Fat posters.

One morning he'd come down to breakfast in a short white robe and a pair of those flimsy, black, rubber-soled slippers worn by Chinese grandmothers, and next thing anyone knew he'd commandeered the basement for nunchaku practice. A pair of nunchakus consists of two short, thick lengths of wood connected by a chain, and enthusiasts whirl them around until they have enough velocity to kill with a single blow to the head. Every time I laid eyes on Dan for the next three years he was a blur of octopus arms, and if I didn't see him, I could hear him, down in the basement: grunting and panting and making the kind of sharp cries a swordsman makes during decapitations.

Far from being concerned, Mom seemed relieved that her youngest son had finally found his niche. One night she and I were sitting in the living room watching *The French Chef* when I felt the hairs on the back of my neck unaccountably rise. I turned to see the deadly missile of a nunchaku whistling past, a half inch from my right temple.

"Ha, ha, madja jump," Danny leered as I shot from my chair with a shriek.

Mom's eyes never moved from the set. "Oh for heaven's sake, can't you play downstairs?" she asked (Dan was twenty-two at the time), and took another bite of popcorn.

*   *   *

Of course it was far easier to look at my siblings' behavior
than my own, far easier to shake my head over the way they
were worrying my parents than to admit I could hardly have
been contributing to their peace of mind myself. However
brief my appearances, it couldn't have escaped them that all
was not well. On one visit, when my mother served chowder
for lunch, my hands and head were both shaking so badly I
couldn't manage a spoon and had to lift the bowl to my
mouth and drink from it like a dog. Another time, bombed at
the wheel of their borrowed car, I accidentally put it into first
instead of reverse and crashed through the garage door. The
two of them were standing in the driveway preparing to say
good-bye. "Sorry!" I yelled out the window, backed out, and
drove gaily away.

They never said much: they were probably so over-
whelmed they didn't know where to begin. Every time I went
to put out the garbage or hang up a load of clothes (of course
I always remembered to bring my dirty laundry), Dad would
be sitting in the breezeway, muttering, "When I was their age,
I had a wife, kids, a mortgage!" or "They can't even scrape
up gas money!" Though outwardly calm, Mom was beginning to cave beneath the pressure, too. She'd become phobic
about germs, rendering the always scanty food supply even
more inaccessible by clipping the wax paper liner in the
saltine box with a clothespin, wrapping cheese in a double
Baggie gripped with rubber bands, and storing leftovers in
airtight plastic containers with masking tape labels: WIPE

DOWN TOP, BOTTOM AND SIDES BEFORE REFRIGERATING; CLOSE <u>TIGHTLY</u>.

Never at her best in the summer heat, she'd also developed an elaborate theory of cross-ventilation, a kind of poor-man's air-conditioning. Every time I turned around she was lowering all the shades to three-fourths of an inch above the sill, or raising all the windows on the east side of the house, or setting up fans in the middle of the room where people would trip over them.

The whole scene made me extremely nervous, though I didn't stop to think this may have been because by that point everything made me nervous, or that someone who was drinking up to a quart of hard liquor a day *should* have been nervous. All of it—the drinking, the sleeping around, the wasting of what I knew on some level was a precious, precious life—gnawed at me constantly. Typically schizophrenic, I'd flagellate myself one second ("Mom and Dad are obviously thoroughly disgusted and discouraged with me . . .") and lash out the next ("They <u>smother</u> me! I swear if they had it their way they'd be privy to every last sick detail of my life. They are just so <u>nosy</u> and <u>concerned</u> it makes me feel like I'm suffocating . . .").

I pretended I wasn't hurting anybody but myself, but more and more when I saw my parents, I began to see I was lying. They were so decent and honest, so hardworking and plainspoken and good to their neighbors, that their very existence seemed a reproach. It was terrible to look at them and think of everything they'd given me and that this was how I was repaying them, that this was the example I was setting for my brothers and sisters, that every morning I was going to go out and spit on my birthright once again. In fact, my entire life—my stance toward sex, work, my place in the world; the gap between how I wanted to be and how I really was—was so dishonest and selfish that if I'd really taken a look at it I would have imploded.

I tried to contribute when I went home—jokes, good cheer, presents when I had the money—but all I could really do was take. I bought my father a sterling-silver razor from Shreve, Crump & Low, then accepted another two-hundred-dollar check when I left. I bought my mother a journal made out of handmade Italian paper, when the real gift, for all of us, would have been to quit drinking and look for a job. I took their food, took up room, sucked what warmth I could out of them, and then crawled back to Boston, sick with guilt. Deep in my heart, I knew that was the best thing I could contribute. It was better, for everyone, that they didn't see me.

twenty-seven

Will you forget us forever?
Will you leave us abandoned day after day?
Turn us back to you, O Lord,
and we will come to you.
            —Lamentations 5:20

Save us, Lord, or we shall perish.
Turn us back.
            —Matthew 8:25

The big day had finally arrived: I was graduating from law school. My impulse was to simply boycott the ceremony, but my parents had received an invite and since they'd financed a good part of the last three years, I figured the least I could do was show up, too. Naturally this required major lubrication. At seven a.m., massively hungover, I started drinking Buds. At nine, I switched to vodka. At eleven, I called Town Taxi, stopping at Macy's for a bottle of Moët and

Chandon, hoisting it from the backseat and telling the cabbie my life story on the way to Hynes Auditorium. "You take the reshht," I said as we pulled up to the curb, shoving the remainder of the bottle at him along with a five-dollar tip of my father's money.

In the lobby, groups of happy students were excitedly hugging their families, signing one another's programs, having their pictures taken. I spotted my parents and Geordie in a corner, all spruced up and peering hopefully around.

"This certainly is a special occasion!" Mom greeted me.

"Nice goin', Heath," said Geordie.

"Look at that," Dad said, pointing to my name on the program. "Cum laude, what's that mean?"

"That's for the extra-smart ones, Dad," I smiled, half sarcastic, half I'm-still-your-girl.

"I always said cream rises to the top," he said proudly.

"Yeah," I said, and for a second, I would have given my right arm to have been the kind of person he really could have been proud of; the kind who really was rising to the top, instead of sinking to the depths of slime and mire.

"You'd better get going, hadn't you Heath?" Mom said.

"Whoa," I said, looking around to find that my classmates had disappeared, "meet you afterward," and I stumbled off to shoot the breeze in the dressing room, take a clandestine nip or two from my purse, and trip across the stage to accept my diploma, breathing toxic fumes on the poor, beleaguered dean.

Afterward Dad drove us to Swampscott, a town on Boston's North Shore, for dinner. "I think you'll like this

place," he said on the way, handing a clipped-out restaurant
review over to the backseat. "I made special reservations."
When we arrived, it turned out to be a beautiful converted
inn, with leaded-glass windows and a fireplace in the dining
room, one of those fancy old-time New England restaurants
that serve breadsticks with port-wine cheese spread and
melon balls with sherbet and lobster Newburg.

"This looks great," I said as we settled in. "I think I'll have
a martini." In fact I had several, waving my empty glass at the
waitress with obnoxious over-friendliness as she set down our
entrées.

"How's the job search going?" Dad asked as we dug in.

"Good! Really good!" I lied. "Yup, I've been interviewing
all over the place."

"Must be kind of a tough market," Geo remarked.

"Good thing I did well," I answered, thinking, Not as
tough as my hangovers.

"Will you go in for a certain area?" Mom chimed in.

"Probably civil liberties," I replied, musing, Area? Yeah,
the area right in front of the Smirnoff at the closest dive bar.

"Well that's wonderful. There are certainly a lot of people
in the world who need help."

"There sure are," I agreed, signaling for a Courvoisier and
wondering if I could get them to drop me off at Misty's after.

Over dessert, Mom presented me with a carefully
wrapped box. I opened it, unfolded a layer of purple tissue
paper, and lifted out a black wool business suit. "I got it at
Stearns," she said shyly. "I think it's your size. If not I can alter it." I pictured her shopping, trying to pick out just the

thing that would please me, spending more hard-earned money for her daughter the lawyer.

"Oh isn't that nice," I said, holding it up. "Oh that will surely come in handy!" my insides heaving with the rotten knowledge that the only way that suit was ever going to see the inside of a courtroom would be if I stole a car and/or got arrested for DUI.

I passed the Massachusetts bar that summer, but if ever anyone made a futile effort, that was it. Not only was I temperamentally, emotionally, and practically unequipped for a job in the legal field, I could no longer physically go without a drink for the eight or ten hours such employment would have required. I made a few half-hearted attempts to land a job, showing up hungover for interviews with stockings full of runs and my hair like a fright wig, but these did not go well. Most people all but beg their interviewers to hire them; I all but begged them *not* to. "I don't have any experience," I emphasized to a Ropes and Gray recruiter. "I mean I don't have *any experience* at all." My lack of conviction was infectious. As I was droning on to a partner from some other upper-crust firm, lying through my teeth about working well with others and how there was nothing I enjoyed more than a good challenge, I looked across the table to find that, right in his Brooks Brothers suit, he'd fallen asleep. Having downed a pint of Southern Comfort before lurching my way to the financial district, I must say it was all I could do not to join him.

My world was getting smaller by the minute, and when it became clear I wasn't going to make it as a lawyer, I saw but a single option. I went back to waitressing: this time at a steak house on the edge of the combat zone: Boston's red-light district. Jimbo's was the sort of time-warp place, often found in the fringe areas of dying downtowns, that you walk into and say to yourself, Where do these people live? What do they do? Where have they been for the last thirty years? Shady-looking men in toupees and cheap loafers drank Manhattans in the gloomy lounge, the house specialties were pasty seafood Newburg made of artificial crab and a truly bogus version of frozen beef Wellington, and, beneath the register, a glass case held cigars and pocket-sized tins of aspirin and licorice pastilles, like a hotel out of Raymond Chandler.

The rest of the waitstaff consisted of gay males slightly past their prime. Randolph tied a cloth napkin around his balding head and pranced around the kitchen, demanding to know whether we liked his "babushka." " 'What do I want, what do I want?' " Morgan singsonged, leaning against the bun warmer as he imitated an indecisive customer. " 'How the hell do I know what you want?' I ask them. 'Do I look like I have a crystal ball?' " On the break between split shifts we all walked down to the Tic-Toc Club and blew our lunch tips on drinks, critiquing the drag queens while Cedric, who groomed lap dogs on the side, held forth on how to pocket the money from cocktail, dessert, and appetizer orders, a stratagem he referred to as "creative financing."

I'd been better off, I realized now, *before* I'd gone to law school. Back then I'd been just a run-of-the-mill loser, but waitressing with a law degree was so spectacularly pathetic I felt like a leper. "It's been over a year since I graduated from law school," I wrote in my journal, "and I have applied for exactly one job. That is positively sick. Over 52 weeks and every week I've promised myself I'll get to work on it Monday, for sure, and about 50 weekends out of those I've gotten dead drunk and it's taken me till Wednesday to recover, if I've recovered at all, and the days and weeks and months have slipped by, and now, as usual, I feel like a worthless piece of shit . . ." In an especially gruesome touch, I'd taken to wearing as part of my work uniform (along with one of two red shirts, both of which I'd purchased at the Salvation Army) the black wool skirt from the business suit my parents had given me for graduation. Every hungover morning, I pulled it from my locker, wet a paper towel, and dabbed ineffectively at the scabs of ground-in A1 sauce and ketchup, then sighed, lit a cigarette, and decided my apron, equally dirty, would cover most of it up.

In the midst of a two-week bender, I stayed up all night, showed up late the next day for the lunch shift—the last thing I remember was watching two coffee cups slide slowly off my tray and onto the gravy-caked carpet—and got fired. Changing into my street clothes in the locker room, I stuffed the black skirt into a paper bag and, weaving my way home, accidentally left it on the subway. The other half of the suit, a double-breasted jacket, hung forlornly in my "closet" (a pole suspended from the ceiling with twine) for months. I finally took it down one morning, rolled it into a ball, and shoved it in the deepest, darkest back of my bottom bureau drawer.

Shortly afterward, the unthinkable occurred: Terry, my nursemaid, confidant, and only real friend, decided to move to Nashville to be with Stephen. "That's great, Terr," I said, but deep down I was devastated: it forced upon me the passing of an era that had already been gone for a long time. Part of me was still back at the Den of Iniquity, longing for the closeness of the days when we'd had barbecues in the backyard and listened to Bob Dylan. Other people had moved on, but psychologically I never really had. I'd never really built a life of my own; I didn't know how to.

Now there was no middle ground between Misty's and total isolation; now I lost my way in earnest; now things started getting really nasty ("The sun is setting and I am seized with a curious unrest . . . of course there is basically nowhere to go, nobody to go with, and no money with which to do it, though this won't necessarily stop me . . ."). I started drinking morning, noon, and night; I started getting drunk more than once a day. When I came to in the morning and there was nothing left from the night before but a glass of warm beer with cockroaches floating on top, I scooped out the cockroaches and drank the beer. When I came to and the sky was an indeterminate gray, I called the operator to find out whether it was six in the morning or six at night. One night I finally went too far, wung an ashtray at Pinhead and got temporarily kicked out of Misty's.

After that, I really started hitting bottom: I started hanging out at JT's Place, a coffin-shaped men's bar across from Boston Garden that reeked of Lysol, opened at eight a.m., and was frequented by drinkers so advanced in their careers they looked as if they might keel over and die from cirrhosis right on their bar stools. "It seems to be a prerequisite to drinking or working in this high-class establishment to be missing at least one tooth," I observed in my journal. "I think JT's stands for Just Totalled." At night JT's was rowdy, packed with Celtics or Bruins fans who swilled beer and broke bottles over one another's heads, but the morning crowd, beaten down and subdued, was a different matter altogether: old men who woke up in shabby bachelor apartments, slapped their stubbled cheeks with Aqua Velva, and pulled on a pair of Ban-Lon slacks to go out and get sloshed in.

It was like coming together each morning for the administration of a communal anesthetic. Our fingers shook with the effort of lighting cigarettes. Our hands shook as we raised the glasses to our lips. Our heads shook when we lowered them to sip. We drank silently, methodically, the pace as steady as an I.V. drip. I was almost always the only woman at the bar, not that it mattered: we JT's regulars were by and large way past sex. We were like monks or eunuchs, our lives stripped down to a single all-consuming, self-annihilating passion, our focus on the bartender mixing our morning drinks as pure as the gaze of the faithful as the priest raises the consecrated Host.

After a few rounds (boilermakers for them; for me sea breezes: grapefruit and cranberry with bar vodka so raw I'd have to hold my breath so as not to throw up), our nerves would have steadied enough so we could "talk." Every morning it was the same cast of characters: Louie with his faded Semper Fi tattoo, John with his psoriasis and long yellow nails; every morning the same TV shows: *Jeopardy!*, *Wheel of* (*Bad*, I always mentally added) *Fortune*; every morning the same liturgy of lame gags.

"It's so cold out I saw a chicken with a capon," Louie would say every day of winter.

"Working hard or hardly working, heh-heh," John would say every day, period.

"What time did I leave yestiddy?"

"Boston Cab came and carted your ass off around eleven."

"Eleven! Where the hell was I till nine last night?"

"Buddy said he seen you over at the Tam after buying rounds."

"The Tam! No wonder I'm cleaned out! Between here and there, blew a C-note and a half . . ."

"How long'd you last, Counselor?" someone called down the bar—Counselor, when it was all I could do to sit up straight for a couple of hours, never mind function as a lawyer—but I'd already tuned out. Behind the bar the Crown Royal lay shrouded in its blue felt bag, the Midori glowed a sickly green, the brown bottle of Seagram's 7—geriatric booze that evoked solitaire, V.A. hospitals, colostomy bags—huddled on the bottom shelf. After *Sale of the Century*, I did the crossword—squinting now; I was starting to see double—arranged my change in piles, and spilled my drink (Why couldn't I ever remember to eat?), soaking my dirty dollar bills in chemical-smelling vodka while, for the hundredth time, someone told the story about the St. Paddy's Day when Louie won the trifecta at Suffolk Downs, and for the hundredth time someone else said, "We musta closed up every bah in Reveah *that* night . . ." If I could still walk, I'd make my way down to the far end and blow a few bucks on pinball, the flippers recalcitrant, my reflexes off by half a second. In the ladies' room, I'd stand swaying in front of the mirror, licking a finger and trying to wipe off last night's mascara, thinking, Man, do you need a haircut.

Afterward, I'd put some money in the jukebox. I love you so much it hurts. I'm lookin' for Blue Eyes; has anyone seen him? Ten o'clock on a Tuesday morning in a shithole bar and already I was so wasted I could hardly stand up, already my day was over, already it was time to head back home—past the sugar-and-coffee reek of Dunkin' Donuts, the fat cigar-smoking men in overcoats, the Mafia place with the fruit baskets wrapped in yellow cellophane—stumble upstairs, and pass out.

My eyes ranged over the room for a minute—the stain on the wall, the dust under the bureau, the phone that never rang—before they closed. Send me the pillow that you dream on, so darlin', I can dream on it, too.

JT's had a resident caretaker, a kind of modern-day Quasimodo. Larry was the kind of person teachers might point out to schoolchildren as an example of why *not* to start drinking. When I first saw him, hanging around morning after morning, mopping the floor, restocking the beer, I thought, Oh that's cute, there's a seventy-year-old man with a ponytail. Then I learned that Larry was thirty-eight. Larry had gray hair, about four teeth, and a voice like Walter Brennan. "Hey, ya wanna do a line?" he'd wheeze, swiping the bar with a dirty rag.

I thought I spent a lot of time in bars, but Larry was one up on me: he *lived* in one; he actually had an apartment in the basement of JT's. I went down there once, none too steady on my feet at that, and from what I remember it was something like the cabin of a boat, but that may be because my brother Geordie was with me and he's worked on boats all his life. Geo has blue eyes and a bashful smile, and is one of those all-around good kids who grew up to be an all-around good adult about whom hardly anyone ever has a bad word to say, and if they do, they're jerks. Also, he is probably the best storyteller in my whole family, which is saying something. He has a scary story about the time his foot got tangled in fishing line and he went overboard and almost drowned, a funny story about the time he ate too much chicken on the boat and had to hide that he was gagging because he didn't want the crew to think he was seasick, and a truly great story about the time he was trying to strike up a conversation with a girl he'd met in the Laundromat and a pair of his raggedy underwear flew out of the dryer and landed at her feet.

Anyway, don't ask me why I brought this wonderful brother of mine to JT's, except that he was visiting for the day and at the time it was the only place besides my apartment I ever went. "Wait'll you see the lowlifes at this place," I told him (like I wasn't one myself). "No, seriously, you gotta get a load of these characters."

So I dragged him down to JT's and ushered him in. In the gloom, Larry was sloshing dirty water around the floor with a stringy mop.

"Eeuuww," Geordie said, "what's that smell?

"Who knows?" I told him. "Puke, come, rotting corpses . . . Larry, meet my brother."

Larry looked up from the mop bucket, strands of greasy hair pasted to his forehead, his eyes like bloodshot hard-boiled eggs. "My sympathies," he said, extending a dripping hand. "You grew up with *her*?"

In any case, there we were sitting at the bar a few drinks later, and Larry, bless his soul, wanted to make it nice for us by inviting us down to his place for a few. Or maybe he just felt like talking to someone halfway sentient for a change, which at that point would have been anybody but me.

"Follow me," he offered. So we all filed downstairs and squeezed into this tiny room with a cot and a metal folding chair and about fifty cases of beer in it. "What'll it be?" he asked, opening one of those dormitory-sized refrigerators. "Heineken, Guinness . . . let me tell ya, workin' in a bar has its advantages. . . ." Being in such close quarters, I could smell Larry's whiskey-barrel breath. It wasn't bad breath–bad breath usually comes from teeth and Larry hardly had any–it was just distillery breath (mine, no doubt, was mountain-spring fresh).

"Yeah, jeesh, Lar, this is real nice of you," Geo said, smiling uncertainly, as Larry broke out another six-pack.

At some point we wended our way back upstairs to the bar, and the rounds kept coming–"Your brother's okay," people kept saying; "Hey, man, your brother's good people"– and the cigarettes kept burning down, and the hour hand on the Schlitz clock moved from five to eight to one. I'd so wanted to show Geo a good time, but as usual the night ended in fiasco. I ran out of money, so Geordie had to pick up the tab; I got on one of my crying jags, so Geordie had to comfort me; and, on the way back up to the loft, I fell on the stairs, so Geordie had to half carry me up and put me to bed (the next day my legs were covered with bruises so dark they were almost black—I'm pretty sure I was in the beginning stages of scurvy).

When you drink alcoholically, you never have *fun*. You might occasionally have hilarity, but fun comes from energy, inner strength, emotional health. Geordie represented fun, and I think Larry and I both sensed that. Because for weeks afterward, every time I walked into JT's, Larry would look up from his filthy mop bucket and ask wistfully, "When's your brother coming down again?"

twenty-eight

My dwelling, like a shepherd's tent,
is struck down and borne away from me;
you have folded up my life, like a weaver
who severs the last thread.

—Isaiah 38:12

Merrimac Street might have been bearable for an actual artist—two working painters had converted the whole sixth floor to a *real* loft—but as a falling-down, blackout drunk it was almost unbelievably depressing. People slashed at each other with razors, every full moon meant a broken window or two, and the arson squad was constantly evacuating everyone in the middle of the night because some nutcase had started a fire in his wastebasket.

Blacky, my next-door neighbor, had lived in the same apartment for sixteen years. Blacky was a fifty-two-year-old alcoholic with an ax-shaped purple face, no teeth in his lower jaw, and nine cats who circulated between his sty-like room and the hall, where hair piled up along the baseboards and drifted into the corners like snow. These were not regular cats, the kind who chase birds or jump up in people's laps, but *Village of the Damned* cats, silent cats with weirdly blank eyes who lurked in the corners and watched your every move, like private detectives.

One morning, as I made my way to the communal bathroom, one of my lamentably bare heels landed in a huge, soft, orange-brown pile of some ungodly, disgusting feline mess. I ran to the sink gagging, washed off my foot, gagging, and yelled, gagging, down the hall, "Blacky! There's a big gross pile of cat shit out here!" Then I went back to my book. An hour later, I went to use the bathroom again. Hearing me, Blacky ran to his door.

"Heather!" he cried. "Were you talking about down the hall, near the bathroom?"

"Yes I was!" I snapped. "Do you have to remind me?"

"That wasn't shit," he announced triumphantly. "That was *puke!*"

Blacky and I had always been "friends"—for my twenty-ninth birthday he had given me an empty Avon perfume bottle, a plastic Negro doll, and a flowered cup inscribed with the word "Florida"—but it was after Terrence moved to Nashville that our relationship really blossomed. He introduced me to Thelma, a motherly bottle-blond from the second floor who kept a gallon of drugstore vodka under her bed and sold it by the glass or peanut butter jar, like moonshine. He hooked me up with Peewee, a retired jockey who doled out single cigarettes for a dime apiece from room 312. I had the kind of hyped-up metabolism that jolted me awake before dawn no matter how late I'd passed out, and though I could never get it together to keep booze in the apartment, Blacky drank at home and he always had a stash of rotgut gin or generic beer on hand.

So when my shrieking nerves woke me at four or five or six a.m., I took to knocking on Blacky's door. Sometimes he sold me a sixteen-ounce Pabst or two, and sometimes he felt like starting the day early himself and invited me in. The room would be barely light, and the tip of my cigarette would be glowing in the semidarkness, and Blacky's giant herd of cats would be slinking around in the shadows like lions on a ghostly plain. We'd sit—naturally, the place reeked—a blanket over the window: drinking beer, complaining about Paulie, rating the neighborhood Laundromats. For breakfast he sometimes broke out a can of Spam or a jar of miniature cocktail franks, some fake meat product he bought with food stamps and that would look very much like the mound of Nine Lives quivering about three inches from my chair.

One morning, I went to rouse Blacky for my morning beers and found him instead lying passed out in the hallway. "Blacky!" I said. No response. I nudged him with my foot. No response. I was horrified: not because he might very well be dead but because JT's didn't open for three more hours and I didn't have anything to drink. It crossed my mind to call for help, but I felt vaguely that Blacky and I were not entitled, the way other, more useful citizens—bill-payers, churchgoers—were, to avail ourselves of community services like ambulances. After stepping over his inert corpus for two more days (it's a measure of the caliber of my floormates that I was the only one remotely "together" enough to have even thought of taking action), I finally dialed 911. The paramedics got him out in a matter of minutes, leaving behind a tangle of tape and gauze.

He came home three weeks later, a crutch under one arm, his other in a sling.

"Blacky!" I said when I spotted him limping around the hall. "Where have you been?"

"Brigham and Women's," he replied, referring to a local hospital. "I guess I was passed out lying on my arm for so long, I have permanent nerve damage. Yep, ole Blacky's got a bum wing."

After all the mornings he'd come to my rescue, he would suffer, till the day he died, for my incompetence, my dillydallying, my unconscionable neglect. How could I tell him how sorry I was, how bad I felt?

"Oh Blacky," I began. "That's *terrible . . .*"

"You saved my life!" he said, waving me off with his good hand. "Come on over and we'll have a few Pabsts."

That March they blew up the Madison, a hotel a few blocks away. The morning it was scheduled, everybody at Merrimac Street made their way to the sixth floor, climbed the rickety fire escape, and gathered on the roof to watch. People brought lawn chairs and Spackle compound buckets to sit on, and someone passed around a box of day-old donuts, and someone else had a portable radio. We stood around in knots hunched against the cold, our breath forming clouds, our reddened fingers clutching cigarettes and cans of beer. Thelma was there, and Ralph with his three black mutts, and Blacky, who was already half in the bag. Everybody had on old bunchy sweaters and ripped nylon parkas and wool caps with cat hair all over them. I was wrapped in my down sleeping bag, sipping Almaden Mountain White Chablis from a coffee mug.

Down below, cop cars crawled like toys, ant-like men ran around putting up orange cones, and walkie-talkies crackled warnings: *The street is closed! Stand back!* The hotel was a tall tan pillar with hundreds of windows and, across a little peaked roof, red block letters spelling out MADISON. We talked and sipped our drinks and stamped our feet, and finally, over the radio, the countdown began: Ten, beat, nine, beat, eight . . . Everyone got quiet and watched transfixed: a giant boom, a second of silence, and just as it was beginning to look as if it hadn't worked, the facade crumbled, smoke rose in billows twenty stories high, and the whole building crashed down, sinking to its knees like a man who'd been shot. Tens of thousands of windows and ceilings and doors blown to smithereens, years of work gone in thirty seconds.

"Wow," someone said, and someone else said, "What the . . . ?" We stood there for a while in the cold morning air, and then we all picked up our lawn chairs and Spackle compound buckets and filed silently down the fire escape, back to our separate rooms.

twenty-nine

This is your hour when darkness reigns.

—Luke 22:53

I'd always prided myself on my ability to function with hangovers that would have laid a stevedore low, but now they immobilized me. ("Once again, I have worked myself into a state of utter exhaustion/inebriation/poverty/shame with my incessant drinking. Mom wrote me last week and for the first time said she thought I was an alcoholic. My inner response was—this is not news . . .") I'd lie in bed like an invalid, everything hurting—my eyelashes, the soles of my feet. ("As usual I am plunged into a bottomless abyss of despair, my plodding slug-like solitary existence having been punctuated by yet another truly horrendous negative experience . . .")

The phone rang, but I didn't answer; my P.O. box was right up the street, but I was too paranoid to check it; I avoided the windows, my nerves stretched so taut I was afraid if I got too close some satanic force would compel me to jump. ("Last night around 11, why I don't know, I was seized with the hideous urge to visit Misty's. Arrayed in full flair, cleavage exposed for all the world to see, I seated myself beside a fellow who could not have been more than 18 years of age . . .") I had a stash of literature for times like these, books I had reread so many times they were like medicine, the covers the color of pills: *Wise Blood* (red), *"The Metamorphosis" and Other Stories* (blue), *Notes from Underground* (green). My existence had shrunk down to a triangle with a quarter-mile border—my apartment, Macy's Liquor, and JT's: there were prison yards with bigger perimeters.

One summer morning, still woozy from the night before, I wandered downstairs and sank down on the front stoop, wondering whether there was a special part of hell reserved for wastrels and drunkards. The day before, I'd hit a new low: I'd passed out like a wino on a bench in Kenmore Square. I'd told myself I was just tired, but the truth was I had taken the subway to some cesspool of a bar on Mass Avenue and drank so many gimlets I'd lost count, then I had gone to Kenmore Square, found a bench, and passed out on it like a homeless person. Homelessness, as a matter of fact, didn't seem nearly as untenable a concept as it had at one time. More and more I saw it was just a short step, and actually quite a logical one, from stumbling exhausted down the sidewalk and simply collapsing and staying there, with no further thought than procuring a blanket and a bottle.

Just then, Vinnie came over. Vinnie was the parking attendant from the crummy lot next door, an eighteen-year-old from East Boston with the prematurely rotting teeth of a teenage meth addict.

"Youse seen the rats in the Dumpster back there?" he asked.

"Yeah, at night they're like maggots."

"One crawled out a minute ago, thing was the size of a fuckin' collie."

"No shit," I said, craning my neck for a look.

The driver of a white Lincoln Continental pulled up and laid on his horn. "Aw Christ, what does this asshole want?" Vinnie said, handing me the joint he'd been smoking, and walked off to park the guy's car.

Over on Causeway, the sun beat malevolently down on the orange and green Li'l Peach sign; across the street, a group of chess players mopped their faces in the shade of the Lindemann Mental Health Center; greasy perspiration beaded the back of my hand, like moisture on old cheese; and it came to me that the city was in the midst of a heat wave. The street was a mass of molten tar, and above it shimmered a layer of wavery light. As I sat there—hungover, sweating, stoned—suddenly I saw an apparition. Suddenly, out of the molten tar, rose the figures of my mother and father.

I'm not sure there are words in the English language to describe how little, at that moment, I desired to see my parents. If I'd made a list of all the people in the world in order of desirability of interaction, there would have been the names of the four and a half billion other people, a gap of about a mile, and then, at the extreme bottom, the names of my mother and father. They'd never seen the hole where I lived—who knows how they'd even found it?—and to be ambushed like made me feel exposed in a way that made every nerve ending shriek. I felt like I might throw myself to the ground and grab their ankles, or blurt, "I need to be in a mental institution!" or break out in maniacal cackles, like the murderer in Poe's "The Tell-Tale Heart."

Dad had on a plaid shirt, pants with a crease in them, and a generous helping of Old Spice. Mom wore polyester slacks, Cobbies, and a jaunty scarf pinned to her blouse.

"How do!" she said, as I dropped the joint and clumsily tried to cover it with my zori. "Thought we'd just pop in and see what you were up to."

"You should have let me know," I said, "so I could have"— *made sure I was about five hundred miles away*, I thought—"uh, you know, pre*pared*."

"Oh, it was just a spur-of-the-moment thing," she said. (Right; they would have been planning a move like this for weeks.) "You've never shown us your *place*!"

I blanched. "Let's go for a walk," I suggested, and tried to stand up. But here, my father, whose love I had never heretofore doubted, revealed himself as a traitor: "I have to use the toilet," he said plaintively. I briefly considered saying I didn't have one, but even in my addled state, I knew this wouldn't wash. They had me cornered, like one of Vinnie's Dumpster rats. I was going to have to take them upstairs and show them my loft.

Inside, the fetid pall of cigarettes and wet dog hung over the stairwell like a miasma; urine pooled in unlit corners; and from behind some faraway closed door came a strangled cry of torment. Walt from the fourth floor, wearing a hat made out of a folded-up paper bag, passed us coming down. I tried pretending I didn't see him, but of course he would have to stop. "Find your keys all right the other night?" he boomed, giving my shoulder an avuncular pat. "Gave me quite a start finding you passed out on the landing like that!"

On the fifth floor, Blacky's herd of cats roamed the hall, and Art, a new arrival from the Lindemann with a Civil War fixation, marched up and down brandishing a miniature Confederate flag. I held the door open and let my parents through. Patsy Cline and George Jones albums, scratched beyond repair from where I'd walked over them with slush-caked boots, littered the floor. The pink blanket they'd given me for Christmas when I was nine half covered a bare mattress. Beside it lay an unwashed Stouffer's chicken pot pie pan, overflowing with cigarette butts.

"You've got lots of room," said Mom gamely.

Dad was checking out the refrigerator, which contained a bottle of maraschino cherries, a bottle of tamari, and a jar of Gulden's mustard, all at least three years old. "What do you have for *breakfast*?" he asked with alarm: to my parents, the failure to eat half a grapefruit, several strips of bacon, and a stack of pancakes before sunup was the surest possible sign of severe emotional imbalance.

"I've been so busy working I haven't had time to shop," I lied. "I usually get a donut."

"A donut! That's all you have for breakfast?" he exclaimed. "Jeesh, that wouldn't be enough to hold *me*."

"A donut!" Mom chimed in. "Breakfast is the most important meal of the day! You should be eating something more substantial than a donut."

I hung my head, watching a cockroach emerge from the shadows of a basin of dirty dishes and make its way around the rim of a brandy snifter I'd ripped off from some long-forgotten restaurant. Were they kidding? Did they seriously imagine breakfast was my problem? Breakfast! I hadn't had breakfast in *years*! I drank vodka for breakfast, I ate beer nuts for breakfast.

"Where's the bathroom?" my father wanted to know.

"Why, it's down the *hall*, Dad," I chuckled, as if that's the way they did it in the city, "and don't forget your T.P.!" I handed him a roll—you couldn't leave anything in there or someone would steal it within seconds—thinking of the slimy shower, the crud-encrusted sink.

He returned, looking a little green around the gills. "Who was that in the hall with his fly open?" he asked.

"That's Blacky," I said, a bit defensively. "He sometimes drinks a tad too much" (understatement of the year, and like I didn't) "but he's actually a very good neighbor."

I think that was when my parents knew I'd truly lost it. For a moment, they simply stood and stared, their faces etched with pity.

"Anyone hungry?" Mom asked. It was only eleven-thirty, but I knew they were raring to go for lunch. Besides, a restaurant meant the blessed opportunity to drink.

"Starving," I replied.

We walked over to Ponte Vecchio in the North End, where Dad had always loved the veal parm. But even three carafes of Chianti couldn't drown out what I'd just seen through their eyes. This wasn't some kind of temporary lark I was on, a phase I was going through. This was my life.

thirty

The Father spoke from all eternity just one
Word. And he spoke it in an eternal silence.
And it is in silence that we hear him.
                                —St. John of the Cross

It was awful living without Terry, but at least we still talked
once or twice a week. "You sound tired, honey," he said
next time he called. "Why don't you come down to Nashville
and take a little rest?"

Oddly enough I was "between jobs" at the time, having
been fired from one more crappy restaurant since my parents'
visit. And since Terrence was offering to spring for the ticket,
I thought I'd take him up on it, even though I knew it would
make me feel like a pathetic charity case. I really was tired—
more tired than I'd ever been in my life. What with the constant need to find the money to drink, and scheme for the
next drink, and actually drink, I felt like a slave in one of
those Ben-Hur movies, dragging a pallet of boulders: strain-

ing, sweating, the lash flaying my bloodied back. Things had
gotten so bad I was embarrassed to tell some of the worst of it
even to my beloved Terry.

A sense of impending doom now permeated my every
waking and sleeping hour: as I boarded the flight, I realized
this wasn't a vacation, or even a visit in any accepted sense of
the word: I was just taking my body to some other place to
bide its time before it gave out, or I had a complete nervous
breakdown, or the universe decided it had had enough and
somehow found a way to exterminate me. When we hit some
turbulence on the descent, I had a moment's reprieve, hoping
that the plane might crash, but no such luck. It touched down
without a hitch, and Terry was waiting at the gate to whisk
me back to Stephen's family compound.

It was August, hot and humid. "You want the A.C. on,
honey?" he asked in the car.

"No, but I could use a cold drink."

"Those are mimosa trees, the ones that are all pink."

"Mmm, mimosas," I said, barely looking out the window.
"Do you guys have any champagne?"

I'd been down to Nashville many times before, with Terrence, and staying on Stephen's spread really had always
made it special. His family owned hundreds of acres of un-
spoiled land, right within the city limits. Nashville had grown
up all around them, but Stephen's father still lived in the same
stone house he'd brought Stephen's mother to as a bride fifty
years before; still had dinner every Sunday with Stephen's
Uncle Louis, who lived with his family in another corner of
the compound; still walked a hundred feet down the dirt

drive each morning to the white clapboard cottage he'd been born in, which was now the office of the family rendering plant business.

Up until recently, Stephen had been living with *his* brother Louis. But Terry and Steve had spent the past year building their own place, a spacious log cabin on the east side of the homestead. They'd finally moved in: in fact, I was their first visitor. Stephen was waiting at the door: hale, hearty, and black-Irish-handsome as ever. "Welcome to the new Greazy Valley!" he said. "C'mon, we'll give y'all the tour. Yonder's a big ole patch where daffodils grow in spring, and that's cardinal creeper climbin' over the windows . . ."

They went on to show me the Mexican sunflowers, the magnolia trees, the birdhouses they'd put up to attract purple martins. I oohed and aahed and said, "Wow, that's really something" and "What a treat," and as soon as they were done, I settled into my upstairs bedroom, unpacked the paper bag I'd brought as a suitcase, and started drinking almost around the clock. When my hosts arose in the morning, I was already reeling at the kitchen table with coffee and Tía Maria. Afternoons, I swilled wine. I blacked out before dinner and fell off the porch. The most I could manage was to make dinner conversation and occasionally dry the dishes, but even that was only a front so I could keep on drinking. "Boy, this summer heat goes right to your head," I explained—as if things would have been one bit different in winter.

Every morning, Terry drove downtown to his job as a gofer for a personal-injury lawyer, and Steve walked across the field to the office in the hollow where he and his Aunt E (who lived in yet another part of the homestead) kept the accounts for the family business. I would have been mortified to be working for my family, but Stephen seemed to love his job, and even though Terry complained about his, he was at least contributing to the general welfare. Alone back at the house, I, naturally enough, felt like a complete parasite. In fact, I felt so bad about myself I could have gouged out my own eyes: the meaninglessness and uselessness of my life, the hell I'd woken up to day after endless day, month after month, year after year; the fact that in some perverse way I was imposing it all on myself, were borne in on me with such intensity I literally felt like I was cracking up.

Drink in hand, I paced from room to comfortable air-conditioned room, fretfully riffling through the shelves full of books and records, the cornucopia-like pantry, Terry and Stephen's overflowing clothes closet, painfully aware of the gap between their lives and my own skid-row existence. It wasn't just passing out in the hallway and washing my dishes in a bathroom sink; emotionally I might as well have been living in a cardboard box and scavenging food from a trash can. I kept casting around in my psyche for a stray scrap of strength, a crumb of resilience, but I had no resources left. How was I going to take care of myself when I got home? How was I going to function? When Terry asked me to drive to the store one day, I shrank back as if from a flame. A strange neighborhood, a strange car—I'd get lost before the end of the driveway, have an accident. He took one look at my stricken face and said, "That's okay, come keep me company. I'll drive."

"Y'all want to go to Bill's Catfish House?" Steve asked anxiously when he got home from work, as if I were a convalescent whose appetite and interest needed to be kept up, which wasn't that far from the truth. So he and Terry drove me to Bill's, where we got a table overlooking the bayou, and ate catfish and hush puppies and sweet potato pie. They drove me on back roads to the Loveless Café, where we had country ham, and biscuits with peach preserves, and we drank iced tea on the porch, with the smell of honeysuckle drifting past our rockers. They drove me to a plain brick house on the far side of town, where an old black guy had a smoker in his yard, and bought two cardboard cartons of barbecue—one mild, one hot—that we took home and sopped up with Wonder Bread and coleslaw.

I could have wept, they were so kind and solicitous, except that alcohol had so successfully drained me of every emotion but self-loathing that I couldn't feel much of anything: there was so little left of what constitutes a human being it was as if I'd been embalmed and forgotten to lie down. The thoughts in my journal had whittled themselves down to one subject: "The temptation I have been <u>powerless</u> to resist all my adult life—the one which has been responsible for virtually all of my misery, the one which has made me a failure, which has largely shaped my reputation and character in the cruel, unflinching eyes of the world—is, yes, the deadly demon ALCOHOL: my nemesis, my Armageddon, my albatross, the noose around my neck, my personal skull-and-crossbones. I hate to keep dwelling on it, but I must, for it has <u>literally</u> taken control of my life . . ."

My visit was drawing to a close. One afternoon shortly before I was scheduled to leave, I wandered outside and, fidgety with nervous exhaustion, decided to take a walk. Cigarette in hand, I made my way past the vegetable garden and cornstalks and hayricks. At the far edge of the back field was a stand of pine. I headed toward it, jumped a stone fence, and walked in: the cool hush of the shade, the carpet of needles soft beneath my feet, tiny twigs crunching. It was so quiet I could hear the beat of my heart, and it made me realize how seldom I was really alone, how afraid I was to be with myself. I was so bone-tired it was an effort just to stand up, and next thing I knew, I'd slithered to my knees beneath one of the trees. I rested my forehead against the flaking bark, breathed in the clean smell of resin. A clump of gray-green lichen bloomed; ants swarmed the trunk like black stars: wondrous things I had lost the capacity to wonder about. I touched and smelled and stared, trying to work up some kind of emotion, and I couldn't. I'm dead inside, I thought. If I don't stop drinking I'm going to die.

I'd always been the first to scoff at paranormal experiences, but the very next instant I felt a force—there is no other word for it—physically pulling me down. It was like entering a kind of fifth dimension: for a split second I "saw" heaven and hell; good and evil; the terrible battle being waged for people's souls. One was being waged for mine, and the netherworld was winning. I didn't stop to think. I instinctively did what had never once, in all my years of drinking, occurred to me to do before. I opened my mouth and said: "Our Father, who art in Heaven, hallowed be Thy name . . ."

I hadn't said the words since Sunday school, but there they still were, within easy reach: "Thy will be done . . . Give us this day . . . Forgive us our trespasses . . ." When I got to "Deliver us from evil," I repeated it several times. I'd always thought of people who believed in evil as religious crackpots or Christian fundamentalists, but I was suddenly very clear on this: by evil I meant drinking.

What was it but evil that I was obsessed with something that was killing me? What was it but evil when I longed with all my heart to be good, useful, loved and was compelled to do this thing that made me feel bad, exiled, hated? Drinking was destroying me, and I didn't know how to stop. Of my own free will, I couldn't stop. With all my supposed intelligence, I was going to die before I stopped. "Deliver us from evil!" I implored loudly, as if speaking through a door to someone I wasn't sure was there. "Deliver us from evil," I whispered, burying my head in my sweaty, shaking hands.

I half expected some celestial being to descend from the heavens on a ray of light, but nothing happened. Shadows dappled the forest floor, cicadas sang from the upper branches of the trees, but I didn't hear a voice, didn't see a vision, didn't feel transformed. "Did I just . . . pray?" I wondered aloud, my usual self-consciousness returning. Then I got up, walked back across the field to the house, and mixed another pitcherful of gin-and-tonics.

Still, something weird had happened in those woods and, sitting on the porch with my familiar props of Tanqueray and Winstons, I knew it. I thought of telling Terry when he got home that night, but I didn't know a single person besides my mother who ever prayed, and in the end I decided I'd only look like a bigger lunatic/loser than I did already. It *seemed* like a big deal—but it couldn't have been if I was drinking again five minutes later.

I kept on drinking, all the way back to Boston, to my job at Sam's Seafood Shack, to the day of my father's birthday party, but I couldn't get that afternoon out of my mind. For a minute, I'd almost felt like one of those characters in a Flannery O'Connor story—Hulga, watching the charlatan preacher make off across the field with her wooden leg; Mrs. May, who'd been impaled on the horns of a bull. But no, that was stupid: their moments of truth had been violent, sudden, cataclysmic. All I'd done—and even then only because I'd been too weak to hold it up—was bow my head.

thirty-one

They were singing a new song.

—Revelation 5:9

I was half-dead with fatigue and frayed nerves, but as Danny and I drove north out of the city, I tried hard to be vivacious, filling the front seat with plumes of toxic cigarette smoke, bawling with laughter, and thanking him profusely for the trouble I was putting him to.

"So what's new with you?" I thought to ask somewhere around Saugus.

"Can you roll down the window?" He seemed a little tense.

"Oh sure, sorry," I said, flicking my Winston out onto the turnpike.

"It's not the cigarettes," he said. "Have you been drinking?"

"Is the pope Catholic? Of course I've been drinking," I said, rattling the ice cubes in my travel mug. "I'm drinking now. What do you think this is, Pepsi?"

"Well take it easy, will ya? It's Dad's birthday. Everybody's . . . waiting."

"Well excuuuuuuuuuse me," I said, thinking, If I get through this night without an I.V. drip and some bed rest, it will be a miracle, and he's on my ass because I'm having a *drink*?

I sulked past the Leaning Tower of Pizza, Frank Giuffrida's Hilltop Steak House, the Topsfield salt marshes.

"How's work?" Dan tried to make conversation.

"Fine."

"Have you seen any movies lately?"

"No."

Then in my usual sappy way I started to feel bad—remembering a drawing he'd once made me of a girl in a field picking flowers, and how it couldn't have been easy having been born into a family with three older brothers and sarcastic me. I relented at the Hampton toll booth. "I've got it," I said, magnanimously digging into my pocket for a quarter.

We took a right on Exeter Road and then a left at the blinking yellow light and, at the top of the rise, pulled into the driveway of the old homestead. The lawn was neatly trimmed, as always; the front steps swept; and, though I didn't think about it too much, things looked awfully quiet for a party. I'd expected to find my siblings hanging out on the breezeway: telling stories, swapping one-liners, sharing a single small bag of Wise potato chips. Where was everybody? I wondered idly, as I walked into the kitchen and headed for the refrigerator. Behind me, I heard the familiarly heavy footfall of my mother.

"Hey, Mom," I said, popping a deviled egg into my mouth. When she didn't answer, I turned around. Standing beside her was a stranger: a woman with the calm, antiseptic look of a nun. She was wearing Peds, Dr. Scholl's sandals, and a pale-blue cotton cardigan.

"Heather?" Mom said firmly, gripping my upper arm in a steely claw. "I'd like you to meet Trish. Trish is an alcohol counselor."

My heart skidded to a halt, every cell in my body screaming RED ALERT! An alcohol counselor! What was she doing here? Was she here for *me*? An *alcohol* counselor!

"Oh, so you finally realized you have a problem, Mom?" I had the presence of mind to guffaw—my mother had had about eight drinks in her entire life—but neither Trish nor my mother seemed to think this was very funny. Trish extended a hand, the nails filed to smooth white ovals. Mine, as always, were bitten raw: my shirts were all bloodstained near the hem from being wrapped around my hemorrhaging fingers like tourniquets.

"Dad and I and the rest of the family are very concerned about your drinking," Mom continued, as if reading from a script. "We've asked you here tonight to talk about it, and Trish is going to help us."

Too late, I looked around and noticed there were no signs of a party: no streamers, no food laid out on the table, no milling guests. Joe had materialized in the doorway, hanging sheepishly back, and looking like Benedict Arnold.

"I don't know, Heath," he said, shuffling his feet. "I mean . . . well, maybe you *should* slow down a little."

"If that isn't the pot calling the kettle black," I said, casting him a look mingled with bitterness and panic, but even as the words issued from my mouth, I had to admit he had never sunk halfway as low as I had.

The dining room was empty, so, with Mom tailing me, I ventured into the living room. Big mistake. Dad, Geordie, Dan, and Meddy were sitting silently in a circle of folding chairs—I felt like Anthony Perkins in the movie version of Kafka's *The Trial*—each clutching a handwritten paper.

"Oh hi," I said, looking at a point just above their heads.

"Hi," they mumbled back, looking at the rug.

I had no idea what was in store, but I was sure I would badly need to smoke through it. So while my mother handed out glasses and a pitcher of lemonade, I went back to the kitchen for an ashtray. Joe was still standing around hanging his head, his face bearing such a conflicted expression of embarrassment and concern, his eyes so clearly begging *Please don't hate me*, that I secretly forgave him on the spot.

"You gotta be shitting me," I said, rolling my eyes in the direction of the living room.

"You think that's bad," he replied eagerly, "they've got me guarding the door in case you try to escape!" We shook our heads in commiseration before I went back in.

I took the one empty seat, the orange wing chair at the head of the circle, and looked around this room in which we had watched countless episodes of *Leave It to Beaver* and *The Andy Griffith Show*, spent countless holidays, had countless fights, and cracked countless jokes. Everything was the same—the lily-pond watercolor over the sofa, Dad's 1954 softball trophy on top of the TV, the bookshelves with their volumes of Robert Frost, Emily Dickinson, *Karate for Today*—yet everything had changed. My family didn't "communicate"; we didn't talk (except behind one another's backs); we didn't confront. Never before had anyone exhibited behavior even remotely resembling the forthright acknowledgment of *any* problem, much less one as mortifying and shameful as alcohol.

Trish raised a hand for quiet. "As all of us but you, Heather, are aware by now," she began, "what we're taking part in tonight is called an intervention, and I'm what's known as a facilitator. Everyone here cares about you very much, and they've also noticed the role that alcohol plays in your life. Over the course of the past few weeks, they've each written a paper describing one or more times when, or the ways in which, your drinking has affected them. Tonight, they'd like to read their papers to the person they've written them to. They'd like to read their papers, out loud, to you."

Oh my fucking *word*, I thought, lighting a fresh Winston off the end of the old one and trying to act nonchalant. I had always longed for my family to recognize my unique genius, always secretly craved their attention, but I'd never pictured it happening like this. I was the one who was always in on the secret. I was the one everyone else came to with *their* problems. How could it be I'd always thought it was my task to save them and now they were saving me?

Mom went first. "When you were seventeen, I received a call one night from the Hampton Beach police. They'd arrested you on a charge of public drunkenness and were holding you in jail. I'll never forget how sad and confused I felt driving down there to bail you out. Where had I gone wrong? I asked myself. What could Dad and I have done differently?" There was more but I tuned the rest of it out, feeling a sudden kinship with those folk who deal with trauma by acquiring multiple personalities they can switch on and off at will.

It was hard to know how to respond in the silence that followed. Should I apologize? Defend myself? Burst into tears and say, "How could you betray me like this in front of everyone?" Somehow none of those seemed appropriate, so I settled instead on a stiff "Thank you."

Meddy started reading, haltingly, then put her paper down, looked at me, and just talked. "Um, one birthday, I think you were like twenty-five, I made you a chocolate cake, you know, the one you like, out of the Betty Crocker cookbook? And you'd been hanging out at the O'Briens' all day, and when you showed up, you were all swearing, and after you blew out the candles, it was like you didn't even care. You just went and passed out in the living room. You didn't even say thank you. We all sat around feeling bad and ate it by ourselves."

"Thanks," I said when she was done, my stomach churning.

"What I remember," Dan piped up, "is that Christmas Eve when you fell in the kitchen and gashed your head on the dustpan and we had to take you to the emergency room for stitches. I mean it kind of put a damper on things . . ."

Geordie rubbed his hand through his hair and glanced up as if to say, "Christ I hate this, but . . ." "That time you brought your friends from Newmarket to go out fishing with Dad, and you all showed up late and half wasted, and when we got out on the river you knocked Dad's Swiss Army knife off the edge, and didn't even replace it . . . I don't know, it just seems like your life is kind of on hold. It's . . . it's not like you've done anything wrong," he wound up. "We're just worried about you."

Every story was worse than the one before, and the worst of it was that, even so they didn't know the half of it. A couple of times I had to restrain myself from saying, "You want to hear a *story*, did I ever tell you about the time . . . ?" But mostly it was excruciating, having it all laid out like that, watching their faces as they groped for the words, knowing they were trying to be as gentle as possible when I wasn't exactly famous for always being gentle myself. I thought of all the trouble they must have gone to; of how they must have been worrying that I wouldn't show up, that I'd storm out, that it would backfire; of how the brunt of it would have fallen on my mother.

My father went last, stopping every few seconds to get ahold of himself. It wasn't just the time I'd crashed through the garage door, the law school graduation (surprise–he'd *noticed* I'd been drunk), the time he and Mom had visited Merrimac Street. With his over-amped nervous system, it was what he'd *imagined*. "Every morning for years," he said, "I've dreaded opening the *Boston Globe*. Every morning I've been afraid I'm going to read that you've been run over by a car, or raped, or been pushed off the Mystic River Bridge."

"Thanks, Dad," I said over the lump in my throat: finally, they were finished.

Now what? my mind raced: was *I* supposed to say something? Perhaps the thing to do would be display a smidgen of remorse. That was it: I would magnanimously admit I had a small problem, promise to "cut back," and send everyone on their way. Instead, Mom spoke again.

"We've bought you a plane ticket and reserved a bed for a thirty-day stay at a treatment center in Minnesota," she said. "You'll be leaving Wednesday."

I almost had a heart attack. Thirty days! Treatment center (whatever that was)! Unfamiliar surroundings, strange people, *no booze?*

"Wednesday!" I exploded. "What am I supposed to do about my apartment? What am I supposed to do about my *job?*"

"Maybe they'll keep it for you," Mom said soothingly. "And if not, well, perhaps with your law degree, you'll want to work someplace *other* than Sam's Seafood Shack when you get out."

"What is it, some horrible kind of nuthouse?" I asked, picturing me and the old men from JT's, wearing johnnies and sitting around in a dirty cellar.

"Goodness, no," Trish chuckled. "It's a state-of-the-art facility with psychologists and clinicians. People from all over the country go there to get better."

"Minne*sota!*" I keened. "You *would* have to find the most godforsaken place on earth."

"It's supposed to be pretty there," my father said. "Lakes, trees . . ."

"I'm not going to Minnesota!" I cried stubbornly.

If it hadn't been for that trip to Nashville, maybe I really wouldn't have gone. But something had happened to me there; something had started to open in me that had been closed my whole life. And now, what with the unprecedented strain of honesty that had just blown through the living room like a breath of fresh air, such a welter of conflicting emotions was roiling inside me that I could hardly think. Could this ghastly evening be some kind of . . . *answer* to that afternoon in the woods? Could that unfamiliar feeling I was experiencing be . . . relief? Could someone as far gone as me actually learn to *live without alcohol?*

Whatever the case, I thought, reshouldering my usual armor, I had to admit things had scarcely been going well as of late. And if nothing else, maybe I could sleep at this place. (How my parents had scraped up the money for such an outlandish luxury didn't, for the moment, even bear thinking about.) But more to the point, as I lit perhaps my eightieth cigarette of the day, it occurred to me that if I surrendered, they might let me have a drink. I held out for a while longer, but my powers of resistance were going down like a row of dominoes, and when Mom hinted at a cache of sleeping bags waiting in the wings, and the prospect of a group campout till I folded, I knew I was beat.

"Okay, if totally ruining *my* life will make *you* all happy, I'll go," I said tightly. "Far be it from me to wreck *your* little plans."

Everyone hooted and cheered and gathered around me, thrilled. "I couldn't ask for a better birthday present!" Dad said, his weary hazel eyes shining. "It'll be better this way, you'll see." Mom slipped away, her careworn face abeam, to get the food ready. Trish enfolded me in a professional "hug," and said, "This will be the start of a whole new life."

I went rigid as a block of wood, wrenched away, and declared loudly, "I need a drink. I might get the D.T.'s if I don't drink. I should be under medical supervision if I'm not going to drink."

Dad and Trish exchanged glances.

"As long as you don't overdo it," she cautioned.

I raced to the kitchen, filled three-quarters of a highball glass with Popov vodka, and topped it off with a splash of soda. It was probably the hundred-thousandth time I'd raised a drink to my lips, but this time something was different. This time I knew my drinking had been forever changed. This time I thought, with a kind of tremulous, tentative hope: I might not have to do this anymore.

"You can get away from that door now," I smirked to Joe as I took the first gulp, but the way I punched him in the shoulder and sort of fell into his arms instead, I'm pretty sure he knew I wasn't really pissed.

thirty-two

Because the Holy Ghost over the bent
World broods with warm breast and with ah!
    bright wings.

—Gerard Manley Hopkins,
from "God's Grandeur"

I had hitchhiked alone across the country, toured the bars of Greece solo, and staggered by myself around the streets of Boston at all hours of the night, but right up to the minute I boarded the plane, I could not believe my parents were sending me off unaccompanied to a prairie rehab. At thirty-three, it seemed far more responsibility than I was capable of handling. "If I come back carrying an ax and wearing a Carrie Nation sticker, you'll know I'm in trouble," I said as I hugged them good-bye at Logan. I was trying to act chipper, but it was on the tip of my tongue to wail, "Can you come with me?" grab my mother around the ankles, and drag her on board with me. I'd been maintenance drinking for five or six days, too drained to get or keep anything going beyond a steady, low-level buzz, and as the plane took off and the Atlantic receded farther and farther beneath the clouds, then disappeared completely, it was strange to think it would taper off and then there'd be . . . nothing.

From my window seat, I drank several airline-sized bottles of white wine—they're small, I told myself—and made several long, maudlin entries in my journal: "September 17, 5:45 EST, somewhere above the Great Lakes. This could be a turning point in my life; I don't know. My poor sainted parents are sending me to a drying out clinic in Minnesota . . ." "I'll just say thank you now to everyone who's stood by me, cared for me, paid for me, comforted me, and loved me—who has been at times a very unlovable person—all these miserable years . . ." "I am now finishing what I sincerely hope is the last drink of my life—Bolla Soave wine, for the record . . ."

Then, at the Minneapolis–St. Paul airport, I hooked up with the driver, told him I had to buy cigarettes, and snuck what would truly be (I hoped) my last drink: a vodka gimlet in the lounge. I thought surely I must be the only person desperate enough to have ever committed such a boldly daring act, but it turned out almost everybody did the same thing. On our way out, as a matter of fact, we had to swing by the local drunk tank to retrieve Virginia, a socialite from the Upper East Side who'd flown in the night before, ditched the driver, and gotten so bombed the airport cops had found her stumbling around the terminal in her underwear. She climbed into the van, smelling of rum and Shalimar, one knee of her cashmere slacks ripped out. "Good heavens, what a

debacle," she sniffed. "Do you by any chance have a cigarette?"

It was dark by the time we arrived at the treatment center,
a series of low-slung, modern buildings surrounded by woods
and ponds. During the intake process I was welcomed, relieved of the four-thousand-dollar money order my parents
had given me, and made to fill out a plethora of forms, after
which a humorless man in a lab coat classified me as a
chronic abuser of alcohol, marijuana, cocaine, amphetamines,
and LSD. How could I be a chronic user of cocaine when I
only did it three or four times a week? I asked myself indig-
nantly as they led me off to the hospital ward.

Here I arranged my books—*Out of Africa*, John Cheever
short stories—donned my pajamas, and sank immediately
into bed, where I stayed for the next seventy-two hours. I had
suffered such excruciating hangovers for so many years, and
had trained myself to endure such stupendous amounts of
pain, that the physical withdrawal wasn't much worse than
any of the numberless times I'd come down off a weeks-long
binge. I was shaky, dizzy, panicked, and suicidally depressed;
my head throbbed; my mouth tasted like it was lined with
bloody cotton; every nerve in my body was stretched to the
breaking point; my muscles were bunched in knots; oily
sweat oozed from every pore; my breath was like Sterno—but
I felt that way all the time. If anything, I couldn't believe how
lucky I was to be lying down: usually in that state I was at
some grotesque restaurant trying to wait on tables.

I clutched at my books, and fell into fitful sleep, and woke
up sweating, and drank some juice, and slept some more: deep,

leaden, dreamless sleep from which I woke to feel like I was
still asleep; I could have slept for a year. Before, whenever an
uncomfortable feeling of any kind—worry, confusion, grief—
had threatened to raise its ugly head, I'd just have another
drink. Now, the time of reckoning had come, and with it, an
emptiness, an eerie calm. It wasn't just alcohol I was with-
drawing from, but the whole strategy of escape it represented;
I felt stunned, like a cow amazed to find itself too exhausted
to present itself one more time for a hit off the prod. Picking
at the burned-orange bedspread, pondering the hopeless
shambles I had made of my life, I saw I would never laugh
again, never make friends, never have sex (it didn't occur to
me that I had not had any of those things, in any meaningful
way, for years).

Nurses monitored my vital signs, and offered me nerve-
calming Librium, but I toughed it out chemical-free. Partly
this was my Yankee training, partly shuffling around in a
psychotropic-drug-induced haze just wasn't my thing, and
partly I *wanted*, for once, to feel; wanted, instinctively, to experience whatever needed to be experienced. Still, I sensed
immediately that even the simplest decisions would pose a
challenge without the cushioning anesthetic of booze. The
prospect of walking to the smoking lounge, for example,
plunged me into a maelstrom of anxiety, and I deliberated for
many minutes over what to wear, whether to bring a book,
and what to say in the event that another human being addressed me. Only the craving for nicotine finally drove me to
the colossal leap of faith required to venture from my room.

Privately, though, I was starting to look forward a bit to

hobnobbing with the psychologists. They probably weren't used to interesting cases like mine—a female lawyer sitting on a bar stool at JT's. They probably wouldn't know what to do with someone quite so smart. When they got through with me, I couldn't help thinking, I'd probably add a little something to the literature. When a counselor named Pam came to fetch me the next morning, it therefore came as something of a shock. With her sparkly personality and fake cowgirl outfit—red boots, sequin-appliquéd denim vest—Pam came off more like a Dallas Cowboys cheerleader than a psychoanalyst equipped to untangle the tortured depths of a rarefied sensibility like mine. Chatting away about the rest of the staff, her professional background, and the Jell-O salad she'd made for the Labor Day potluck, she also employed an accent I would soon learn to my alarm was characteristic of the entire middle portion of our country: she pronounced the name Bob as "Baab," like the sound a sheep makes, and Wisconsin, the state where she'd attained her degree, "Wis-cannes-sin," as if the middle syllable were home to the world-famous film festival.

"You'll be in Clare, one of the two female units," she explained, leading me down a labyrinthine series of halls, "Here we goh!" and ushered me through a pair of double doors. Draped over windowsills, milling around chatting, and vacuuming the rug were more women than I'd seen in one place since college. Would I be able to stand them? I suddenly wondered. Would they be able to stand me?

"This is the kitchen," Pam was saying (I refrained from opening the refrigerator door to snoop); "here's the hallway"

(pay phone at the end, I noted–very important); "and this is
where we all gather": a huge sunken living room filled with
sofas, comfortable chairs, and a conference table. Virginia,
looking elegantly emaciated in an angora sweater set, strolled
through bearing a fresh set of linens. "Darling, you survived,"
she greeted me, waving a bony hand. "We have to fix your
hair!"

"You're right over here," Pam said. "Grab your bag." I'd
been hoping for a roommate very much like myself: same
general age, same clothing sense, same sensibility. Sitting in
the corner was an ancient woman in a paisley dress and a velvet shawl. "This is Millie," Pam announced. "Millie's a poet
from Wyoming."

The rest of the day was a blur of orientation, meals, and
group interactions. It didn't take me long to figure out which
gals I liked best and bond with them. Naomi, a trust-fund
baby from Boston, had delicate, fawn-like features and arms
covered with angry red track marks. "My parents have had
me locked up so many times I've lost count," she admitted,
pulling down her sleeves when she caught me staring over
dinner. Suzanne was a single mother of two, a nurse from
Minneapolis. "*Used* to be a nurse," she corrected herself. "I
lost my license for stealing the patients' Vicodin." Mo hailed
from an Arizona trailer park, and padded around wearing
terry cloth slippers and a sleeveless housedress with rickrack-
edged pockets that held a tube of dark-red lipstick, hankies,
and a pack of Chesterfields. "Hi, mah name's Mo, and I'm
addicted to booze *and* pills," she opened that night's gathering
in a rawhide drawl.

It was the first such gathering I'd ever attended, and when they started going around the room and introducing themselves I almost died. It was straight out of some fifties days-of-wine-and-roses melodrama; I couldn't believe people actually said this stuff in real life. "Hi, I'm Naomi, I'm an addict." "Hi, I'm Greer, I'm an alcoholic/addict." "Hi, I'm Heather, and my family thinks I'm an alcoholic," I said when it came to me.

Everybody cracked up laughing—music to my ears—but of course Pam had to wreck it. "Heather," she interrupted gently. "There's a reason we identify ourselves as alcoholics. It's an admission of powerlessness. It's a way of saying we need help."

What a jerk, I thought. And how stupid could I have been to think some corn-fed counselor would understand *me*?

The subject of the meeting was trust, and in spite of my big mouth, when push came to shove I ended up being too shy to say anything. But it did get me to thinking that I knew a thing or two about trust myself. "Last night we talked about trust," I wrote in my journal the next morning, "and it finally dawned on me—no wonder I don't trust anybody. My life could definitely be conceived as one long episodic series of betrayals of the lowest sort—beginning with Allen Bigbee cheating on me, right on through Terry abandoning me for Stephen, and culminating in my staunchest companion—alcohol—turning on me and my own family leading me like a lamb to the slaughter to sit me down in my own beloved living room to tell me I have a drinking problem and that I'm leaving for Minnesota on the next available plane. You're fucking-A right I don't trust people—would you?"

Naturally it didn't occur to me for a minute to wonder how trustworthy I'd ever been myself.

I'd pictured a kind of resort spa, but instead our schedule was packed with household chores, writing assignments, and lectures. Every morning at ten, we filed into the auditorium for a talk by a doctor, therapist, or ex-boozehound. I'd hoped to hear that the well-balanced adult I would have been, but for the fact that I drank eighteen hours a day, would soon come to the fore. Instead, to a person the speakers maintained that alcoholism was a mental, physical, and spiritual illness that called for a radical overhaul of one's entire life. I was at least starting to be able to buy that, but when I got a load of the purple-and-gold slogan-bearing banners—"One Day at a Time," "Live and Let Live"—festooning the walls, my heart sank. I didn't want to be a snob, but for someone of my sensitivity, my sophistication, my . . . complexity . . . no, such an approach would never work for me.

Still, as four days passed, then five, then six, there was no rational explanation for the fact that I was no longer drinking. What was the miracle of the Virgin Birth or the Resurrection of Christ compared to the fact that I—who until recently had been incapable of going more than a few hours without alcohol—*no longer had the craving to drink*? Basic things like making my bed in the morning and putting on pajamas at night filled me with a novel sense of accomplishment. I woke before dawn, bundled up in a sweater, and walked through the woods. Yellow leaves carpeted the ground; the sun broke crimson through the trees. One morning near the end of the first week I came across a pond, where a blue-gray heron with long, stick-like legs regarded me through the mist. He was so beautiful I wanted to thank him. Back home at that hour, I would have been drinking sea breezes and inhaling the smell of Lysol from the mop bucket at JT's.

That afternoon I went to the bookstore (which, to my initial disgust, consisted entirely of "recovery" literature) and, looking around to make sure nobody was watching, purchased a small black volume of daily meditations. In the privacy of my room, I examined it closely. It contained *Reader's Digest*-type thoughts about living in the present, acceptance, turning one's life and will over to the care of God.

How could I turn myself over to someone about whom I knew nothing? How would I do it even if I wanted to? Bring your body, and the mind will follow, they said in the lectures. He always hears an open heart, they told us. So I made it part of my daily routine to come back early from breakfast and, on my knees by the bed, mouth the words to prayers I barely understood and hardly dared hope would ever be heard.

By the middle of the second week I'd quit highlighting all the cornball phrases in the book they'd given us—"boiled as an owl," "John Barleycorn"—and started to actually pay attention to the speakers they brought in from the outside. I'm not sure who else I thought alcoholics might be, but many of them seemed to feel, think, and act, if not look, very much like me. One night some guy from upstate New York who'd been through this very treatment center fifteen years before walked up to the podium. He wasn't someone I would have ordinarily felt I had anything in common with—middle-aged, suit and tie, a glad-handing CEO type. But when he started talking about his drinking, I identified with every word: the insanity of doing the same thing every night; the blackouts; the lost jobs and opportunities; the lying and excuses; the conviction that, because he was halfway intelligent, this time it would be different, this time he'd figure it out.

He was married, and one night he and his wife had been to one more party where he'd blacked out, once more she'd driven home, one more morning he'd come to, hungover, feeling like killing himself, and he had been forced to ask his wife what he'd done and said the night before. It was the same as a thousand other mornings, and when his wife was giving him the thousandth postmortem, she'd turned to him and asked: "Aren't you sick of *missing* everything?" That had gotten his attention: not that he'd stopped drinking right away, but it had gotten his attention.

And it got mine, too: something about the way he told it stopped me cold. Because that was exactly it: I was really really sick of missing everything. I had just about missed my whole life.

Back on the unit, we had significant-event sheets to fill out, personal inventories to write, and grief group to attend. "You're only as sick as your secrets!" Pam chirped, and urged us all to "share."

This will be a big bore, I thought, in my usual open-minded way. Instead people shared—which is just another way of saying they told their stories—and, against all odds, the stories were riveting. Virginia had passed out at her daughter's ballet recital. Naomi told of pawning her baptismal ring to buy heroin. Millie described dyeing her vodka blue and hiding it in the Windex bottle. "I useta stash mah scotch in a rubber douche bag and hang it over the towel rack," Mo said. "Ever'time my old man went in there to pee I 'bout had a coronary thinkin' he might find it."

The stories had all the richness and detail the stories in law school had lacked. They had honesty and vulnerability; they had pathos, humor, narrative thrust. But more than that, they told me these women were as desperate and tormented as I'd been: they told me I wasn't crazy, I wasn't unique, I wasn't alone. Joan was a housewife from Iowa, Yolanda a supermarket checker from Miami, Greer a Yale drama student— but it wasn't the differences that made themselves felt; it was the similarities. We had in common the same guilt, shame, despair; we shared the same spiritual bankruptcy. Virginia looked about the best of any of us, and up close even she had the telltale splotchy skin and tremulous hands of a nervous system on permanent overload. My impulse in any group was to compare, establish my place in the pecking order, convince myself I was either better or worse: instead, all I felt was compassion. In a sterile meeting room in the middle of rural Minnesota, I began to glimpse the feeling I had looked for all those years in sleazy barrooms: a sense of fellowship, belonging, home.

Not that I wanted to get all sappy about it or anything. The stories were often punctuated by heart-wrenching crying jags, and though I was glad to press a tissue upon a grieving comrade, I did not cry myself, even when I told about the morning drinking in old men's bars, the bruises from falling down in blackouts, the shame of slinging hash as a licensed lawyer. Oh for God's sake, why make it worse, I thought grimly, and cracked another joke.

One afternoon Pam drew my attention to a painting mounted on the back wall of the meeting room, one of those kitschy clowns with an oversized red smile and a tear coursing down one cheek. "That reminds me of you," she said, shaking her head. "Laughing on the outside and crying on the inside."

I rolled my eyes, crossed my arms a little tighter over the front of my Jack Daniel's T-shirt, and, as soon as Pam's back was turned, made a gagging motion across the room at Naomi. A *clown* painting! If that wasn't retarded, I didn't know what was.

In such close quarters, there was no hiding our idiosyncrasies. Millie snored like a lumberjack, Virginia was bulimic, and my own mercurial moodiness was accommodated but in no way encouraged. The spirit was of not being judged but not being coddled either. You were acknowledged without being singled out as special, needed, but not clung to; and if you helped out it was appreciated but nobody was going to give you a medal for it. For someone like me, to whom "right-sized" was but the vaguest of abstractions, this all came as a revelation.

At the beginning of my third week, Pam appointed me

house mother. "I can't be an authority figure," I protested. "I *hate* authority." But she made me do it anyway, and secretly, I was just the teensiest bit excited at the prospect of running the meetings and organizing weekend activity hours.

Saturday afternoon, we were all in the kitchen cleaning cupboards when a woman from a local church dropped off a stack of hymnals.

"Okay, I'm the boss around here," I announced. "Who wants to sing?"

A chorus of girlish squeals went up: "*Pam* never makes us sing!" "No *way*! They made fun of me in school." "Count me out, I couldn't carry a tune in a suitcase."

A mannish voice cut through the babble: "They tell me *I* don't sound s'bad." I looked over. Mo had one hand on her hip. With the thumb and fourth and fifth fingers of the other, she held a broom handle. The remaining two gripped a Chesterfield, stained ruby at the tip.

"Thank you, Maureen," I said. "I'm glad to see someone around here is willing to participate in her own recovery."

"I'll sing soprano," Naomi piped up.

"I'm alto," rumbled Mo.

"You're more like basso profundo," I said, "but we'll make do."

We started out with "Praise to the Lord" and gained a couple of new voices on "Holy, Holy, Holy." "That's the spirit," I urged them on. "Who gives a shit about the kitchen?" By the time we got to "All Glory, Laud and Honor," half the unit had set aside their sponges to join in. A bunch of us launched into

"Gloria in Excelsis Deo," which was above Mo's range, and Mo taught us a hymn I'd never heard before:

> *Boisterous waves obey Thy will*
> *When thou sayest to them, "Be still."*
> *Wondrous sovereign of the sea*
> *Jesus, Savior, pilot me.*

Even the non-singers were impressed. When I suggested charades after dinner everyone joined in without a peep, and we all had such a blast I let everyone stay up past their bedtime.

That night I lay awake a long time. They'd told us it would take weeks for the alcohol to work its way out of our systems completely, and I could believe it. My nerves had been ratcheted up so high for so long it was only now, marginally calmer, that I saw how close to the breaking point I'd been. My hands had stopped trembling and they were no longer a sickly purplish color. My eyes were starting to lose their hunted, haunted look. My thoughts were slightly less obsessive, running slightly less in their compulsive ruts. I was starting to have other kinds of thoughts, snatches of insight such as that in trying to create my own little universe of controlled suffering, I'd also been shutting out joy, sanity, light. It was as if some evil spirit were slowly but surely being driven out. Maybe detox was just the modern word for it. Maybe they should call what really happened at these places an exorcism.

*   *   *

Suzanne, the Vicodin-addicted nurse, was scheduled to leave on a Wednesday. That Tuesday, I was in the office mooching an envelope when Pam came in carrying an object made of white tissue paper and balsa wood that, upon closer inspection, turned out to be a butterfly.

"That's queer," I observed helpfully. "What's it for?"

"It's for Suzanne's ceremony tonight," Pam explained with her usual maddening patience. "Every girl gets one the night before she leaves. It's a symbol of transformation, of how during your time here the old you . . . falls away and a new one emerges." Apparently she mistook my look of disbelief— what next? rainbows? unicorns?—for interest. "Go ahead and write a message on it," she said, handing me a pen. "You know, something for Suzanne to remember you by."

"Sought through prayer and medication to improve our conscious contact with God," I wrote with a snicker, ostentatiously crossing out the "c" in "medication" and replacing it with a "t"—then passed it on to Virginia.

That night we gathered in the living room, everyone said something kind and encouraging, and Suzanne gave what even I had to admit was a very moving good-bye "share." Then, not content to leave well enough alone, Pam had to present her with the lame paper butterfly.

"Leave it to Pam to dream up something like that," I bitched to Millie from my bed later. "I mean, Suzie's the best and I hope she makes it and everything, but God. You'd think we were five years old."

* * *

I'd complained the whole time I was there, but deep down I was terrified to go back home. It was easy to feel cheerful here, where there were people to joke and commiserate with, but what about when I got back to Boston? I was a loner, I did everything by myself: I just couldn't imagine doing any kind of regular activity with other people, or joining a group. Sylvia, the hairdresser from Misty's, called one night and said, "It was *time*, Heathah, it was time." She was right, but the problem was that I had nothing with which to replace drinking—no support system, no practical skills, no life experience beyond waitressing and reading. There was my law degree, of course, but I did not hold out much hope of ever entering the confrontational world of litigation now. In the sober light of day, even *agreeing* with people made me nervous.

I was way too proud to say so, and my parents couldn't have afforded it anyway, but I would have done anything to stay another month. (Naomi was going to a halfway house, but her parents were loaded.) In spite of my anti-group bias, the truth was that what went on here had started to interest me. It interested me that even though we supposedly had a disease, the idea wasn't to sit around feeling sorry for ourselves: it was to shoulder responsibility for our mistakes, take moral stock, make amends. It interested me that we broken-down screw-ups seemed to be able to help one another in a way that well-groomed, well-meaning professionals like Trish and Pam couldn't. It interested me that in the flesh-and-blood presence of these other girls, with their cigarette breath, their chipped fingernail polish, their track marks, something was happening to me. Because whatever else came down, however I ended up doing it, one thing I knew: anything would be better than going back to the way things were. The sleazy bars, the squandered hours: it was hard to believe that something so attractive could have simply lost its appeal. That was what was weird. It was like part of me had died. I kept mentally feeling around for it and it was gone.

The morning of my last day, I woke to mixed feelings of dread, sadness, and excitement. I'd never been good at good-byes and this was going to be a big one. I went to the morning lecture thinking, This is my last lecture. I went to the meeting afterward thinking, This is my last meeting. That afternoon I packed my bags, exchanged addresses, and took one more walk in the woods.

I fooled around over dinner—my last dinner!—with the gals and smoked a cigarette on the patio under the stars. Then Naomi and I went to her room to listen to our favorite Tom Petty tape and wait for the Big Event—the good-bye ceremony—to begin.

"I'll get in touch as soon as I get back to town," she said. "Call me out here if you start feeling like you want to drink."

"I can just see a paper butterfly hanging on the wall of my loft," I fretted, poking my Winston through a smoke ring. "One look at that feeble thing would make anyone crave a cocktail."

Finally, there was nothing more to do but trail down to the living room with the others and take my place at the head of the table. "Shall we open with a prayer?" Pam asked, and then, one last time, we all took our turn. "You've been a wonderful roommate," Millie quavered. "You barely complained about my snoring at all." "Don't lose your sense of humor," Naomi said. Mo chain-smoked, announced, "I'm addicted to booze *and* pills" in her own special way, and told me I should join a choir. "Open up! Take risks!" Greer said. "You're a bright, creative person with so much to offer," enthused Yolanda. "I loved you from your first day on the unit." Even Pam chimed in with, "You've tried hard. We all wish you the very best." Out of the corner of my eye, I saw a large white object fluttering beneath her chair. "Would *you* like to share now?" she prompted.

I'd secretly planned out a little speech, a careful blend of wit, jokes, and good-soldier bravado, and I was just about to launch into it when I had one of those life-changing moments of truth. I'd been afraid they'd forget: I'd been afraid they wouldn't *have* the butterfly ceremony for me. That was when I looked at all those faces shining in the lamplight, opened my mouth, and started bawling so hard I could barely breathe: huge hyperventilating sobs, with big hot tears, that wracked my body with such force I thought it might break. A pair of arms wrapped around me, a hand stroked my hair, someone else ran up with Kleenex, and I just sat there gasping and snorting and heaving, like someone who's been crawling in the desert for a long long time and has finally sighted water.

"I'm *sober*," I wanted to tell them. "All I ever wanted was to not feel so alone . . ." "We're all part of the same . . ." They were simple, childlike thoughts, not complex at all.

I never did say much that night. "Who's up for gin rummy?" Mo barked presently, breaking out a deck of cards, and from the other end of the table, Virginia flourished a bottle of Million Dollar Red and cried, "Won't someone *please* do my nails?" Safe in the circle, I was content to sit quietly—pondering the joys and sorrows of the real world, the mysterious resurrectability of the human heart, the strange new life that lay ahead: drinking it all deliriously in.

epilogue

We must all be saved together! Reach God
together! Appear before Him together! We
must return to our Father's house together. . . .
What would He think if we arrived without
the others, without the others returning, too?
                                    —Charles Péguy

That was eighteen years ago. There have been many more
deserts, seemingly endless stretches filled with sharp
rocks and ornery rattlesnakes and thorny cacti, punctuated
by just enough tiny oases of peace to keep me stumbling
blindly forward toward the next one. The good news is now
I know it's pretty much that way for everybody.

Flannery O'Connor was right: we resist grace because it
means change and the change is painful. It continues to be
painful. I am still just as neurologically geared toward the fix,
the hit, the conflagration as I ever was; just as prone to be
ruled by fear; just as driven by the need for approval, for adu-

lation, to feel better. Recently I asked my sober priest friend Monsignor Richey how I'd know if I was making any spiritual progress. The pious urge to pray many hours a day? I was thinking. Guru status? He pondered for a moment. "If crazy people aren't afraid to come up to you and talk . . . that's a pretty good sign," he said.

If I've made any "progress" it's that now I know I'll be an alcoholic till the day I die, and that that is both my biggest cross and my greatest blessing. Staying sober has proved to be an authentic spiritual path: disciplined, rigorous, and challenging beyond anything I could have imagined. It has led me, at long last, to writing. It has led me to Catholicism. Most of all, it has led me to the city of L.A. and the friends who, day after day, shore me up, show me the path, fulfill the longing as much as I believe it is given to anyone to have it fulfilled on this earth. I've faltered and lurched at every step, but now I know we all pretty much do that, too.

Tommy left three children: if he'd lived, he would have been a grandfather by now—twice. Terry and Stephen have been together twenty-eight years. A licensed social worker in Nashville, Terrence counsels alcoholics, drug addicts, and people with AIDS: we still talk on the phone every couple of months; we still remember each other's birthdays. Billy is married with three children; he travels around the globe working with murder victims' families, for human rights, and to abolish the death penalty. Allen Bigbee is married for the second time, lives on the coast of Maine, and still surfs.

Peter Parks married his high school sweetheart and works for Amazon.com in Seattle. Jill teaches women's studies at a university in Illinois; we saw each other at our twentieth high school reunion and have since drifted out of touch. I haven't talked to Sylvia or Dot, from Misty's, in years, but their kindness, the fact that they stuck by me during one of the longest, darkest stretches of my journey, is a permanent part of my inner landscape.

As for my own family, how can I ever repay them? How can I ever say how much they mean to me? Meredith is a songwriter living in Northampton, Massachusetts, Joe's still touring with his punk-rock band the Queers, Geordie has a wife and two kids and runs his own fishing boat, Jeanne's a nurse in New Hampshire, Skip is a contractor in L.A., Danny teaches ESL in Bangkok. They are the most eccentrically talented, funniest group of people I know, and now that we're no longer fighting over the last pork chop or baking-powder biscuit, it's an embarrassment of riches to have six other people so willing to endlessly reprise the high points of our tragicomic childhoods.

Five years ago, when my father was dying, we all came home. For two weeks, we sat with him: holding his hand, feeding him medicine, telling him we loved him. He died in the living room of the house he'd built for us, and is buried in the Post Road cemetery. Shortly afterward, my mother sold the house and bought a condo in the neighboring town of Stratham. She reads, goes to church, and does good deeds, the way she always has. I still visit every summer and every summer I am struck by her patience, her loyalty, how incredibly well she did by me and how lucky I am to have her.

Today I know that if I turned out all right it's precisely

because of my parents; because they had the fineness of character to show in everything they did to be kind, to be good to your neighbor, to persevere. They gave up their lives for me and my brothers and sisters, never asking for recognition, never implying for a second that it was anything other than what they'd signed up for instead of a staggering, saint-like sacrifice. Their blind faith, unwavering hope, and fierce love are the main reasons I'm still around—and a continual reminder that my task is to pass those things on to others. My father lived long enough to see all of us come into our own, and my mother, in her late seventies, plays with her grandchildren and, I hope, enjoys a modicum of maternal peace.

Boston holds such bittersweet memories, is so emotionally fraught, I hadn't been able to bring myself to visit till last year. I was home visiting my mother in New Hampshire and I took the train down one morning from Newburyport, through Ipswich and Hamilton-Wenham and Lynn. In the distance, I could see Revere Beach, where Terry and I used to go to get our tans. I got out at North Station. Boston Garden was gone, the Celtics and Bruins having moved around the corner to the spiffy new FleetCenter. The whole area was under construction: orange cones, the sidewalks torn up. People were maneuvering their way around: eating donuts, clutching cups of stale-looking coffee, smoking cigars.

I had a couple of free hours and I hadn't been sure where I was going to head first. Now it was as if I'd known all along. As if in a trance, I picked my way across Causeway, still plunged in shadow from the green girders of the old Lechmere line, and walked down a few blocks. Memory is a funny thing. I would have bet my life that it was on the corner, but the sign loomed a couple of storefronts in, where it must always have been: bright yellow with green letters. Irish colors. "JT's Place." I stood there a minute and, with a shaking hand, pushed open the door.

Everything was as I remembered: the stillness, the gloom, the smell of ground-in cigarette smoke, Lysol, death. It seemed a long way to the middle of the bar, where the people were. A hungover-looking bartender, his one foot hitched up on the sink, was talking to two youngish guys, also appearing the worse for wear, nursing long-neck Buds. "Hey," I said. Their eyes moved as I walked by. I went as far as the bathrooms, taking it all in: the jukebox, the crappy paneling, the missing chunks of linoleum where the floorboards showed through. They'd torn down a wall and made an extra room with a pool table in it, but other than that, it looked exactly the same.

I caught a whiff of my perfume: Mitsouko, dabbed on that morning from a ninety-dollar cut-glass bottle. I had on good underwear, black silk from Bloomingdale's. I was going to meet an editor on Newbury Street for lunch. *I used to drink here*, I thought, smoothing my hand over a glass-sized spot worn white on the Formica bar. *I used to get out of bed in the morning and come down here and drink.* My heart was beating so hard that for a second I thought I might pass out. It was like revisiting the hole where you'd once been held in solitary confinement: a force field of muscle-memory-stored pain and toxic energy so palpable I was afraid if I stayed any longer it might suck me back in.

On my way out, I stopped by where the three guys were. I couldn't help it. It was the same urge that had driven me to hang out in bars all along: the urge—in those days, forever doomed to fail—to connect with another human being. "I–I used to drink here," I blurted. "I used to come here every morning and now I haven't had a drink in seventeen years. I–I just had to see it one more time. I'm visiting from L.A. and . . ."

They didn't even look up.

"Okay, then, take care!" I waved, backing up toward the door.

And when I opened it, to the humdrum scene of traffic and sunshine and people, the world had never looked quite so bright.

I still don't know why God allows obsessions, cravings, disease: I just know I'm really glad that when Christ stood among the Pharisees he said, "Healthy people don't need a doctor; sick people do." I just know that anything that is worthwhile about me arose, in one way or another, from the suffering of those twenty years of drinking. I just know that only a God of inexhaustible love, infinite creativity, and a burning desire to count every last one of us in could have taken a broken-down wreck like me and made something useful out of her.

And as the great German mystic Meister Eckhart noted, "If the only prayer you said in your whole life was 'Thank you,' that would be enough."

about the author

Heather King lives in Los Angeles and is a graduate of the University of New Hampshire (1977) and Suffolk Law School (1984). Her essays have been published, among other places, in the *Utne Reader*, the *Los Angeles Times Magazine*, and *The Sun*; and anthologized in *The Best Spiritual Writing 2002* and *Son of Man: The Best Writing About Jesus* (Avalon, 2002). She is a commentator for NPR's *All Things Considered* and a communicant at St. Basil's Church in Koreatown.